Education, Economic Change and Society in England 1780–1870

Second Edition

Prepared for
The Economic History Society by

MICHAEL SANDERSON

Reader in Economic and Social History
University of East Anglia

M
MACMILLAN

First edition 1983
Second edition 1991

Published by
MACMILLAN EDUCATION LTD
Houndmills, Basingstoke, Hampshire RG21 2XS
and London
Companies and representatives
throughout the world

Typeset by TecSet Ltd, Wallington, Surrey

Printed in Hong Kong

British Library Cataloguing-in-Publication Data
Sanderson, Michael
Education, economic change and society in England
1780–1870. — Revised — (Studies in economic and
social history)
I. Title   II. Series
942.07
ISBN 0–333–56342–5

Contents

Acknowledgements

I am grateful to my colleagues, Professor Roy Church and Dr David Smith and also to Professor Christopher Smout and the members of the publications committee for helpful comments and suggestions during the production of this pamphlet.

I am also especially indebted to my wife whose interest and encouragement have lightened the task.

Note on References

References in the text within square brackets relate to the numbered items in the Select Bibliography, followed, where necessary, by the page numbers in italics, for example: [5:27].

Editor's Preface

When this series was established in 1968 the first editor, the late Professor M. W. Flinn, laid down three guiding principles. The books should be concerned with important fields of economic history; they should be surveys of the current state of scholarship rather than a vehicle for the specialist views of the authors; and, above all, they were to be introductions to their subject and not 'a set of pre-packaged conclusions'. These aims were admirably fulfilled by Professor Flinn and by his successor, Professor T. C. Smout, who took over the series in 1977. As it passes to its third editor and approaches its third decade, the principles remain the same.

Nevertheless, times change, even though principles do not. The series was launched when the study of economic history was burgeoning and new findings and fresh interpretations were threatening to overwhelm students – and sometimes their teachers. The series has expanded its scope, particularly in the area of social history – although the distinction between 'economic' and 'social' is sometimes hard to recognise and even more difficult to sustain. It has also extended geographically; its roots remain firmly British, but an increasing number of titles is concerned with the economic and social history of the wider world. However, some of the early titles can no longer claim to be introductions to the current state of scholarship; and the discipline as a whole lacks the heady growth of the 1960s and early 1970s. To overcome the first problem a number of new editions, or entirely new works, have been commissioned – some have already appeared. To deal with the second, the aim remains to publish up-to-date introductions to important areas of debate. If the series can demonstrate to students and their teachers the importance of the discipline of economic and social history and excite its further study, it will continue the task so ably begun by its first two editors.

L.A. CLARKSON
Editor

1 Literacy and Mass Elementary Education

Industrialising societies face many dilemmas. Among these is the balance to be struck between the investment in the industrialisation itself and that accorded to the social infrastructure, including education. Education may contribute directly to industrial perform-ance by improving the technical quality of the labour force. Or indirectly it may, for example, induce a sense of discipline and peaceful order within which industrialisation can thrive. Yet there are counterproductive dangers. Too much may be spent on educa-tion and social investment to the detriment of industrial capital formation, which may lead to a retarding of growth. Some societies have paid attention to achieving high levels of mass literacy while neglecting to produce technologists; others have sought to run prestigious technical institutes at the top end of a society largely abandoned to illiteracy. In the 1868–1914 period Japan would be an example of the first case and Russia of the second. The English industrial revolution from about 1780 may be counted an economic success. Was this success achieved with the help of strong educa-tional support or in spite of serious education defects? Or was it helped by a judicious balance of attention to areas of education which could pay off cheaply, and a neglect of high cost alternatives which could be disregarded with impunity? To examine this let us first consider the debate about elementary education and literacy.

(i) BEFORE 1830: CONFLICTING TRENDS

Literacy is usually measured by the ability to sign one's name on marriage registers which can provide a bulk of homogeneous information over a long period of time [1]. This was especially so from 1754 when a standard form of certificate was instituted by Lord Hardwicke's Marriage Act of 1753. We should be clear, however, exactly what such signatures can tell us and what their limitations are. A signature on a marriage register can tell us nothing of how much more the party could write, nor can we convincingly extrapolate how much he or she could read. But one thing is certain. If a man or woman cannot write his or her own name even for this one special occasion, then it is fair to conclude that they cannot write anything at all. In no sense can they be regarded as literate. In fact, marriage register signatures measure accurately the certain level of illiteracy. What we, for convenience, call literacy is in effect 100 per cent minus the certain level of illiteracy. Accordingly it should be borne in mind that even those classified as literate contain an indeterminate sector of very low literacy indeed. However, this standard is the only one possible for securing a sufficient sample to make comparisons of illiteracy rates over time, between places and occupations.

There is no dispute that in the first two-thirds of the eighteenth century literacy levels rose in England. This is hardly surprising since it was a period of very slow population growth accompanied by a considerable expansion of endowed schools, sometimes called 'the charity school movement' [2]. The Society for the Promotion of Christian Knowledge (SPCK), founded in 1698, encouraged the formation of such schools for the defence of the Anglican Establishment against Catholicism and Dissent. Not all such new schools needed to be in contact with the SPCK and certainly the idea of an SPCK-directed movement lasting the whole of the century is no longer tenable [3]. But it is plain that there was a very considerable increase in new endowed schools in the early eighteenth century, whether or not we term them 'charity schools'. Between 1710 and 1730, the most intense phase of their formation, 23 new endowed schools were founded in Cheshire [4], 36 in Derbyshire [5: 27] and 32 in Lancashire [6]. As the provision of schools expanded more than the population warranted, so the chances of receiving a few years of education increased. This was also helped by a tradition of self-teaching facilitated by publications like Thomas Dyche's *Guide to the English Tongue* which went through 46 editions between 1709 and 1796 [7:73]. Literacy rates rose accordingly. The view that literacy rose in the eighteenth century before the 1760s or 1770s seems at present to be a matter of general agreement. Lawrence Stone has estimated that male literacy in England and Wales rose from just below 50 per cent to 56 per cent between 1700 and 1775 [8].

R. A. Houston has presented the fullest figures for the rise in literacy in England in the first half of the eighteenth century (his figures shown in Table I are converted from illiteracy to literacy figures) [9: *33,60*]. The marked rise in literacy between the later seventeenth century and the first half to three-quarters of the eighteenth century is evident, as is the wide disparity between male and female rates and across the social spectrum.

Table I
Male and Female Occupational Literacy in England 1700–70

| | 1640–99 | | 1700–70 | |
	Male	Female	Male	Female
Professional	97	76	100	100
Gentry	100		100	
Craft and trade	57	22	74	31
Yeoman, tenant	51	12	74	32
Husbandman	25		58	
Labourer	15	5	36	12
Servant	27	15	50	25
Soldier	45		54	
Unknown	38		70	

After the 1760s and 1770s the evidence diverges. In one of the very earliest attempts to calculate eighteenth-century literacy, W. L. Sargent in 1867 found that of a sample of 15,000 people, 51 per cent of those marrying between 1754 and 1762 could sign their names and this percentage rose to 54 for those marrying between 1799 and 1804[10]. This suggested a steady rise from the middle of the century to the end. In one of the first of the modern surveys, W. P. Baker studied 17 country parishes and chapels in the East Riding of Yorkshire from 1754 and found that male literacy was 64 per cent both in 1754–60 and in 1801–10, rising steadily thereafter [11]. This has been taken as evidence of an overall improvement in literacy from the 1750s to the early decades of the nineteenth century, although there is a significant dip in Baker's figures to which we will refer later.

The most important statement of the view that literacy was rising from the 1770s to the 1830s is the major essay by Professor Stone [8]. Stone used the evidence of Sargent and of Baker and added further findings of his own. These consisted of parish register evidence for Penzance, Oxford, Northampton, King's Lynn, Bristol, Nottingham and Halifax, and marriage licence evidence for the Oxford Archdeaconry and the Gloucester Diocese. His town evidence showed that all towns experienced a rise in literacy between 1754 and 1762 and 1799 and 1804, except Penzance which remained stable. Between 1799 and 1804 and 1831 and 1837 all experienced a further rise, with the exception of Northampton and Halifax which declined in literacy. The marriage licence evidence showed that amongst artisans and tradesmen, yeomen and husbandmen, labourers and servants there was a rise in literacy from 1775 to 1800 and in the first four cases to 1825 also. For England and Wales Stone regarded literacy as having risen from around 56 per cent in 1775 to around 65 per cent by 1800 and to 66 per cent by 1840. Stone thus saw 'an upsurge of literacy after 1780' underlying the process of industrialisation and partly due to 'the demand for a literate workforce for an industrialising society'. These conclusions have been taken up by R. M. Hartwell, who finds the literacy studies of Sargent, Baker and Stone in accord with the assumptions of contemporary development economists that education is important for economic growth now as it was also in the eighteenth century. He also holds that there was an increased demand for artisans who could read and concludes that 'there was a notable expansion of education in Britain before the industrial revolution and that the expansion was important in promoting faster economic growth and finally the industrial revolution' [12].

There are, however, grounds for thinking that this may be too optimistic a view for England as a whole. The sharp rise in population from the 1760s to the 1830s, partly caused by a rise in the birth rate, began to swamp the existing provision of schools. There was also a decline in the creation of new endowed schools. Whereas 131 schools had been founded in Derbyshire, Cheshire and Lancashire in the four decades 1710–50, this fell to 81 schools founded in the same area in the five decades 1750–1800. The donors who had put funds into charitable endowments for education in the early part of the century now had more expensive and pressing outlets – enclosure, canal and turnpike investment – to divert their surplus funds. Moreover, much of the religious tension that had motivated the finance of education in the early decades of the eighteenth century had slackened after 1760. The dynamic areas of growth in the education system were no longer the charity schools for the lower orders, but private paying schools for a somewhat higher social class. The grammar schools, too, became more middle-class, fee-paying establishments, as we shall see.

Most important, children were drawn into the new process of industrialisation. Whereas there was very little for a child to do in domestic industry that would occupy him for more than the hour or two devoted to bobbin winding, the factories demanded a long, full day's work. This was especially the case from the 1790s when large numbers of children were needed to assist the spinners of steam-powered mules. Children were also employed in mines, canals and metal working as a result either of technical change or of the expansion of production. As the economic position of thousands of hand-loom weavers deteriorated after the 1810s, so the potentially high earnings of children in cotton factories changed from being a welcome addition to the family budget to being a stark necessity. Moreover, factories could usefully employ children at an earlier age, say 9, than they could start full-time domestic weaving or farm work, say 12, which cut back three valuable years of basic literacy schooling. All this – population rise, decline of formation of new school endowments, increase of opportunities for child labour – militated against working-class children receiving an education that would make and keep them literate, especially in industrial districts. Accordingly, it would be surprising if literacy rates did not sag under these various pressures.

The chief development countering these factors which were unfavourable to literacy was the Sunday School movement from the 1780s. In 1780 Robert Raikes, a Gloucester newspaper proprietor, gathered some children who were idle and disorderly on Sundays and had them taught some lessons in a church. Following this experiment the movement spread with some 2,290 schools in 1801 rising to 23,135 by 1851, and enrolled children rising from 59,980 in 1788 to over 2 million by 1851 [13: *44*]. By this last date Laqueur calculates that three-quarters of working-class children aged 5–15 were attending such institutions. However, there are some limitations to making a strong case that Sunday Schools sustained the literacy rate. Firstly, Laqueur finds their growth only slow in the last two decades of the eighteenth century. Secondly, after sabbatarian disputes in the 1790s many schools ceased the teaching of writing [14]. Laqueur's view that the Sunday Schools were the creation of a working-class culture of respectability and self-reliance has been questioned by those who see them still as middle-class conservative institutions for the reform of their working-class pupils from above [15]. The strength and power of these schools is undeniable in providing some part-time education for children otherwise engaged in factories during the week, and a focus of their social lives. A positive force in a darkening situation, they probably prevented literacy falling more than it did in areas vulnerable to decline.

We may now turn from the balance of circumstantial evidence to the firmer statistical data in which can be detected a fall in literacy in the last decades of the eighteenth century and the first decades of the nineteenth. The data are presented in Tables II and III with the peaks (usually some time between 1750 and 1770) and the troughs (usually some time between 1800 and the 1820s) cited for clarity. There is ample evidence of a sharp fall in literacy in Lancashire and adjacent Stockport presented by Sanderson [6], Birtwistle and Laqueur [16]. The argument is by no means confined to this area, since similar declines are found in work on Leamington Spa [17:*159*] and Devon [18] and even in W. P. Baker's work on the East Riding. This does not present a picture of a forward surge of literacy after 1780. In particular the Lancashire evidence, together with that for Halifax and Nottingham presented by Professor Stone, does not suggest that the industrial revolution was underpinned and facilitated by improving levels of literacy and education before the 1810s or 1820s.

Most important of all are the findings of R. S. Schofield based on his sample of 274 parishes [19]. He found a slight rise in female literacy from just below 40 per cent in the mid-eighteenth century to just above 50 per cent by 1840. For males, however, he found no improvement in literacy at all from the 1750s to around 1815. What Schofield's finding in fact conceals is at least two, and possibly more, quite different trends. There is clearly the declining trend of areas like Lancashire and industrial or merely populous towns. There is also a stable or rising literacy trend of rural areas or towns not experiencing severe social strains. When these divergent trends are aggregated as in Schofield's study, they emerge as a horizontal line. This is sufficient, however, for Schofield to conclude that 'The English experience in the century from 1750 to 1850 may perhaps be taken to cast doubts on the utility of positing universal relationships between literacy and economic growth.'

Table II

Declining Percentage in Literacy Trends c.1760–c.1820: Male

	Peak			Trough	
	1750s	1760s	1770s	1810s	1820s
Lancashire (inc. Stockport)					
Bury (S)	69				32
Chorley (S)		65.7	61		49.6
Deane (S)					20.1
Eccleston (S) (St Helens)	66.2				49.7
Kirkham (S)	76.5			51.4	
Preston (S)	72.7				49.6
Manchester (L)	66.5			42	
Stockport (L)	71.1			51.6	
Bolton (L)	66			37.9	
Industrial Lancashire (L)	67.3			43.1	
Other areas East Riding (WPB)		*1781–90*		*1801–10*	
		67		64	
Leamington Spa (FOS)		*1761–70*		*1781–90*	
		68		41	

Key: (S) Sanderson [6], (L) Laqueur [16], (WPB) Baker [11], (FOS) O'Shaughnessy [17].

The most recent study is that of Stephen Nicholas who has examined 80,000 convicts transported to Australia between 1788 and 1840 [20]. Before departure convicts were questioned as to their literacy skills. This may tend to exaggerate actual levels but gives a very good indicator of trends over time. However, Nicholas convincingly suggests that the occupational structure of convicts was broadly representative of the (non-criminal) English working class. He finds that urban literacy continued to rise to 1808 and rural literacy to 1817 but then both fell consistently for the rest of the period. Moreover, many of the new occupations created by industrialisation were the least literate: 'Britain's industrialisation process was set in the mould of unskilled labour-intensive produc-

Table III
Declining Percentage in Literacy Trends c.1760–c.1820: Female

		Peak		Trough	
	1750s	1760s	1770s	1810s	1820s
Lancashire					
(inc. Stockport)					
Bury (S)		(No trend)			
Chorley (S)	29.2				18.2
Deane (S)		15.2			8
Eccleston (S)					
(St Helens)			26.4		19.5
Kirkham (S)		33.8		23.4	
Preston (S)		43.6		21.7	
Manchester (L)	29			19	
Stockport (L)	27.6			15.7 (1780s)	
Bolton (L)	22			12.1	
Industrial Lancashire	26.3			17.9	
Other areas					
		1781–90		1801–10	
East Riding (WPB)		48		43	
		1761–70		1781–90	
Leamington Spa (FOS)		42		32	
		Aggregated rates			
		1754–70		1800–20	
Blackburn (B)		33		31	
Burnley (B)		29		28	
Clitheroe (B)		50		38	
Great Harwood (B)		37		29	
Newchurch-in-Pendle (B)		34		27	
Whalley (B)		44		37	
		1765–74		1795–1804	
Devon (WBS)		59.6		43.4	

Key: (See also key to Table II). (B) Claude Birtwistle cited in [6], (WBS) Stephens [18].

Note: The literacy percentages for females are somewhat more erratic in movement than those for men. No meaningful trend is evident for Bury women. In Manchester and Eccleston there were quite exceptionally high scores for the 1790s and 1800s respectively but since they were single quirks in an otherwise consistent trend they are not cited here. At Stockport Laqueur finds the trough unusually early. Otherwise the figures for women show broadly the same pattern as that or men over a period when differences in literacy levels between the sexes were becoming somewhat less marked.

tion at an early stage . . . once started, the industrial revolution did not call for increasing literacy levels in the years before 1840.' And in Nicholas's view it did not get it.

W. B. Stephens's compilation of the results of probably all known local surveys up to 1987 is the best overall view so far [21: 6,7). He finds that literacy in towns measured by brides' and grooms' marks moved as shown in Table IV between 1754–62 and 1831–7. A similar compilation for over 400 rural parishes finds all except one increasing their literacy rates between the 1750s and 1830s.

Table IV

	Rise	*Fall*
South West	4	–
East	9	–
Midlands	6*	1
North	4	10

* (though literacy in Worcester and Nottingham fell 1750s–1800s)

Divergent as the views are of Stone and Hartwell on the one hand and of Schofield and Sanderson and Nicholas on the other, there is no real dispute. One has no more to believe that literacy was rising or falling throughout the whole of England during the period 1760–1820 than one has to believe in uniform national movements in the standard of living or the birth rate over the same time. The regional variations are known to be considerable and findings about some areas do not invalidate those about others. The present picture is very far from complete. Indeed it is a jigsaw with few pieces in place, and many puzzles. For to undertake the documentary research to trace literacy movements in even one parish is very laborious; to relate them to precise explanatory local economic and social changes even more so. This is an area where much new research is being undertaken. In the meantime we clearly need to avoid thinking of 'England', especially urban England, as a homogenous unit experiencing 'optimistic' or 'pessimistic' literacy trends before the 1830s.

If, then, literacy was declining in several industrial areas, it raises the question of how far literacy was necessary for industrialisation and the formation of the labour force. A small élite in the new factories was literate – clerks, overseers and mechanics. So, too, were many of the traditional craftsmen like carpenters, masons and wrights. Yet paradoxically the industrialisation in its classic focus of the north-west thrived through some fifty years of declining literacy. By the 1830s barely 30 per cent of the workers in South-East Lancashire could even write their own names and almost all the new factory jobs created by the new technology were successfully operated by sub-literate labour, as were the mines and canals [6]. In weaving, for example, power-loom weavers (female) were only a third as literate as the (male) hand-loom weavers they were replacing. Schofield found that the literacy of textile workers halved between 1754 and 1784 and between 1784 and 1814, and that it declined also for metal and transport workers. He suggested that 'some occupations were still less literate than they had been in the mid-eighteenth century . . . [figures] suggest the possibility that for many males in a variety of occupations literacy did not become more essential as a cultural skill during this period . . . since many of the new industrial occupations recruited a mainly illiterate workforce' [19: 452]. Schofield, Nicholas and Sanderson agree on the limited relevance of literacy for much job performance in the new industrialisation. The industrialisation itself, with its rising population, technical change and demand for children, helped to created an illiterate society. In turn the new technology could operate with an illiterate labour force which it had helped to produce, and economic growth was not impeded by educational retardation.

(ii) 1830–1870: THE DRIVE TO MASS LITERACY

Those who discern a fall in literacy in the second half of the eighteenth century see a bottoming-out, usually in the 1810s or 1820s. From then there is no doubt that literacy was set for a steady rise for the rest of the century, though inevitably with regional variations in pace. Literacy figures were officially published by the Registrar General for each census year in percentages (see Table V). David Vincent has calculated rising male literacy rates by social and occupational groups (in the Registrar General's classifications) (see Table VI) [22]. As another indicator of growth the average number of years of schooling of boys rose from 2.3 years around 1805 to 5 years by 1846–51 to 6.6 years by 1867–71 [23: 573]. Various factors lay behind this, but first we should consider the motives both of educators and of educated which made this possible.

Table V

	1841	1851	1861	1871
Male	67.3	69.3	75.4	80.6
Female	51.1	54.8	65.3	73.2

Table VI

Social class	1	2	3				4	5
			Textile	Potters	Metal Workers	Miners		
1839	100	90	63	58	53	21	58	27
1844/9	96	91	58	50	60	20	62	31
1854/9	96	91	70	56	61	30	66	41
1864/9	100	90	85	61	79	47	71	51

The Churches were concerned with the salvation of souls and the winning back of the irreligious working-class urban populations to Christianity. The Established Church in particular felt itself under attack from a revival of Nonconformity and Catholicism in the 1830s, especially in the north-west. At a more secular level the long period of endemic social unrest from the 1790s to the 1840s, from food riots to Chartism, had created a deep anxiety about order and social control. The school and the teacher were seen as substitute families and parents to re-inculcate civilised behaviour and the respectful deference to position. As Richard Johnson has stressed, 'the early Victorian obsession with the education of the poor is best understood as a concern about authority, about power, about the assertion (or the reassertion) of control' [24: 119]. McCann likewise finds that most education in the disorderly area of Spitalfields had 'the aim of controlling the populace in the interests of social and economic stability' [25: 21]. Similarly in the North Eastern coalfield coal owners created schools attached to collieries in the 1850s. This was seen as a response to the strike of 1844. They also hoped to draw miners' children away from their own private dames schools and self-education which perpetuated the ethos and mores of the working class. Coalowners' schools would reassert social control over the workforce [26].

This social control argument was, of course, an old one dating back at least to Raikes's Sunday Schools, the SPCK Charity Schools and beyond. It conflicted with arguments hostile to the education of the lower orders. These suggested that schooling and literacy would render the poor unfit for the performance of menial labouring tasks. Education would raise their aspirations and make them unwilling to serve their betters as 'hewers of wood and drawers of water'. Even worse, the acquisition of literate skills would make the working classes receptive to radical and subversive literature. This was the essential dilemma: whether to deny education to the poor and so avoid trouble, or whether to provide ample education in the hope that it would serve as an agency of social control. By the 1830s the latter ideology dominated in the minds of policy makers. In particular education was seen as a means of reducing crime, and expenditure on punishment. With the prison system costing £2 million a year in 1847 and the Poor Law £7 million in 1832, any expenditure on education which would keep a child out of prison and workhouse as an adult came to be seen as a social investment. In the 1860s these views were joined by two others which presaged the 1870 Act. The victories of Prussia and the northern States of America suggested that good levels of education contributed to military efficiency. At home the 1867 Reform Act prompted a concern to ensure the education of those who would soon wield political power through the extended suffrage.

It also came to be appreciated that, although education was of limited value for actual job performance, it had important wider bearings on the creation of an industrial society. Education effected psychological changes and helped to break down the isolation of rural communities with their limited horizons. By making it possible for people to be in touch with 'a basic network for information dispersal' (by reading notices at least), it could make them aware of possibilities open to them, of jobs for labourers or products for consumers [27]. Notice-reading would also alleviate the problem of safety in dangerous mines and factories. It enabled the efficient functioning of an urban industrial society laced with letter-writing, drawing up wills, apprenticeship indentures, passing bills of exchange, and notice and advertisement reading. For such reasons a positive belief in the value of education on the part of the authorities replaced earlier assumptions that teaching the poor to read would merely lead to the diffusion of subversive literature and a wholesale flight by the newly educated from menial tasks.

The first factor driving up the literacy rate was the injection of public money for the building and maintenance of elementary schools. This rose in thousands of pounds annual expenditure as shown in Table VII [28: *App. I*]. The money was channelled chiefly into two religious bodies, the Anglican National Society founded in 1811 by the Reverend Andrew Bell, and the British and Foreign

Table VII

1833	20	1850	193	1862	775
1840	30	1852	164	1864	655
1842	32	1854	189	1866	676
1844	39	1856	251	1868	750
1846	58	1858	669	1870	895
1848	83	1860	723		

School Society (1810) which developed from the activities of the Quaker schoolmaster, Joseph Lancaster. The latter was originally nondenominational in intention but increasingly came to represent Nonconformist interests. These bodies raised money to build large schools usually run on monitorial lines, i.e. with the large number of pupils made manageable by a system of monitors relaying instructions to small groups of their fellows. Faced with evidence of defects in school provision especially in the north, the state determined to stimulate school growth by subsidising the societies' efforts initially by an annual grant of £20,000 from 1833. Professor West has recently suggested that the level of investment in such education in 1833 was about one per cent of national income and compares well with the 1920s [29]. In 1839 the grant was raised to £30,000 and its administration placed in the hands of the Committee of the Privy Council for Education with James Kay Shuttleworth as Secretary [30]. The positive role taken by such 'administrators as statemen' – civil servant experts developing policies and taking initiatives – is now well appreciated [31], and expenditure began to soar as grants were extended from limited capital grants for building to equipment (1843), teacher training (1846), and capitation grants for the actual running of schools (1853). Following the Newcastle Commission, Robert Lowe as Vice-President of the Committee enforced from 1862 a system of payment by results (government grants conditional on results in annual examinations conducted by Her Majesty's Inspectors) and cut back on teacher training to try to stem the sharply rising expenditure of the 1850s [32]. This is a familiar story often told elsewhere [33]. The point is that these high and sharply rising levels of government expenditure pumped life into the expanding National and British Societies and drove up the literacy rate even before the beginning of secular schools built and run by local government with rate finance after 1870 [34].

However important the role of the state and the religious societies, some authorities have pointed to the large sector of cheap private education where the working classes bought education for their children outside the church and state system [35]. Laqueur finds that in 1851 there were twice as many private as public day schools for the working class though only one-third of pupils were at these private schools. In Bristol there were about 200 of these private working-class schools in the 1850s and 1860s and Philip Gardner considers that at least a quarter of working-class children received their education in this way [36]. They have been underestimated because they disappeared fairly quickly after the 1876 Act which required a child over 10 to have a certificate of proficiency from a 'certified efficient school'. Very few of these schools were classified by the new School Attendance Committees as 'certified efficient' and this significant part of working-class educational culture dwindled.

Why should the working class have seemingly spurned the new big National and British schools and chosen slightly more expensive, small dame and common day schools? Laqueur considers that their quality has been maligned by publicists like Kay Shuttleworth who advocated a state-financed system. Above all the private schools had no taint of charity or of heavy social control by the Churches. They were not part of an authority system, the parents could regard the schoolmasters as their employees and they fitted in with working-class lifestyles. Laqueur sees them growing up like 'butchers or bakers shops' and 'to a large extent responsible for the creation of a remarkably literate working class' [35: 202].

A major factor in the rising literacy was the creation of a teaching profession for the elementary schools [37]. The National and British

Societies had run their own training colleges before the 1830s. Then from 1839 many Anglican dioceses established colleges to serve diocesan National Schools. The system received its most important stimulus from the Minutes of 1846 which established the training and career structure for teachers. Elementary school children of promise could start as pupil teachers at 13 helping to teach younger children and receiving instruction from the headmaster. After a few years they sat for the Queen's Scholarship that would enable them to attend the new training colleges where the successful became certificated teachers and then returned to the elementary schools. The 1850s thus saw the rapid rise of a schoolteacher class. There were 681 certificated teachers in 1849 and 6,878 by 1859, by which latter date there were 34 training colleges. The formation of a teaching body so rapidly in the 1860s was helped by a shift in the population to a predominance of women and many very able girls from the lower classes must have taken this path. Specially-built housing for teachers added to the attraction of the career and helped to raise and define its social status. The increasing self-consciousness of the profession was expressed in the formation of the National Union of Elementary Schoolteachers (later the NUT) in 1870. As a civilising influence and creator of literacy this development was crucial.

A further important factor was the role of Her Majesty's Inspectors (HMI) [38]. The first two were appointed in 1839 to ensure that the £30,000 grant was genuinely spent on school building and not diverted to building chapels. By a Concordat with the Church of England all National schools had to be inspected by an Anglican HMI. Their duties expanded into more educational roles, examining the pupil teachers and the training colleges, calculating the capitation grants of the 1850s and then examining the children in the subjects on which the grant was based under the Revised Code of the 1860s. They also had a wider importance. They encouraged the replacing of the monitorial system with class teaching, advocated rate support for schools, diffused a knowledge of good literature amongst the schools and collected vast amounts of sociological data on education. Not least their inspections generated a salutary apprehension which kept everyone on their toes. By 1870 their number had risen from 2 to 73.

Four measures mopped up the illiteracy of deprived groups who, left to themselves, would have remained a hard core of ignorance.

23

These were the Ragged, workhouse, prison and factory schools. Ragged schools began in the 1840s, the Ragged School Union dating from 1844 [37]. Their distinctive character was that, unlike the state-supported National and British schools, they charged no fees. They took the poorest, vagabond children for a basic education, depending for their support on a circle of philanthropists, which included Charles Dickens. By 1852 there were 132 Ragged schools in London with 26,000 children, and 70 schools outside London in 42 towns. By 1870 at their peak they had 250 schools in London and about 100 in the provinces. After the 1870 Act most were absorbed by the School Boards and the movement's activities focused on running orphanages and reformatories. But between 1840 and 1870 they were an important, underrated agency dealing with the rock-bottom illiteracy of the most degraded children too poor to come within the orbit of the voluntary schools, grants and HMIs.

Ragged school children were at least at liberty. Those who had lost their freedom and fallen into the safety nets of workhouse and prison had their education guaranteed, the former by the new Poor Law of 1834 and the latter by the Prisons Act of 1823 which made obligatory the provision of schooling for children in the respective institutions. Many workhouses had provided for the education of their children by sending them to local schools. From 1834 they more commonly built their own schools. Kay Shuttleworth, who became a Poor Law Commissioner in 1835, toured East Anglia encouraging these, and secured government funds in 1838 to develop Norwood in Middlesex as a poor law model school.

Finally, the Factory Act of 1833, more successfully than that of 1802, obliged factory owners to ensure that their child workers were receiving a regular education either in a factory school or outside, before being allowed to engage in factory work [40]. This was firmly enforced. It was all the more remarkable in that nearly fifty years before general compulsory education was introduced by the Mundella Act in 1880, the 1833 Factory Act enforced compulsory education on a large sector of free children who would have been deprived of schooling. All these measures were positive discrimination in favour of the most disadvantaged groups of children otherwise too poor or too preoccupied to seek an education that would have secured their literacy.

Mass elementary education was founded on the basic skills of reading and writing and arithmetic. Religion and bible study were equally central to National and British school curricula; more enterprising schools would also include some history and geography. The Revised Code grant changes after 1862, by limiting grants to examination passes in reading, writing and arithmetic, directed attention away from the broader cultural subjects and refocused it on the inculcation of basic literacy skills. From 1867, history, geography and geometry were made grant-earning subjects but languages and a range of science subjects had to wait until the 1870s.

It was important not only to make the lower orders literate but also to enable them to retain and sustain that literacy. The development of a body of reading matter accessible to the masses was accordingly a characteristic of these years. At the school level the SPCK, acting as the publishing arm of the National Society, set up its Committee of General Literature and Education in 1832 to produce school books. The National Society gradually took over from the SPCK and established its own depository in 1845, providing books for National schools. The British Society likewise published secular books for schools from 1839.

At the adult level there was a concern among the propertied classes to provide edifying literature that would divert the minds of the potentially turbulent working classes away from the radical propaganda of discontent. Hence the writing of Hannah More and Harriet Martineau, and Cheap Repository tracts against agrarian disturbance or in favour of Malthusian ideas on population limitation [41]. The SPCK and the Religious Tract Society continued to publish religious anti-infidel tracts. Its Benthamite counterpart, the Society for the Diffusion of Useful Knowledge (1826) (renamed the Society for the Diffusion of Entertaining Knowledge in 1829), issued a library of short treatises on popular science, history and all manner of secular subjects. Such organisations were right to take seriously this battle for the minds of the newly or barely literate. They were trying to combat a strong tradition of radical, even subversive, literature aimed at the same clientele. Tom Paine's *Rights of Man* allegedly sold over a million copies in part numbers; there was the *Black Dwarf* and Cobbett's *Political Register* and a spate of unstamped newspapers in the 1830s defying the 1819 Stamp Act which had sought to limit such publication [42]. Into the market came commercial amusement: Dickens's *Pickwick Papers* (1836–7), Gothic and romantic novels and the railway reading of W. H. Smith.

All purveyors of reading matter benefited from the progressive cheapening of book and newspaper production and the improvement in accessibility [43]. Technical change assisted this with the introduction of steam printing and cheap cloth bindings in the 1830s and 1840s and of cheaper esparto grass paper in the 1860s. So too did the relaxation of government impositions. The stamp duty on newspapers and the tax on paper were both reduced in 1836 and finally abolished in 1855 and 1861 respectively. The average price of a book halved between 1828 and 1853. Books and newspapers became more readily available with the Public Libraries Act of 1850 which allowed the formation of rate-supported municipal libraries. If all these matters facilitated reading, the initiation of the Penny Post in 1840 may have had a similar stimulating effect on writing. Per capita delivery of letters rose from 4 in 1839 to 32 by 1871 [22: 39]. They provided an incentive to acquiring literate skills and a means of keeping them fluent.

The work of the Churches and especially the National Society had provided much of the education which had driven up the literacy rate over the mid-century. By 1870 there were 8,798 voluntary assisted schools of which 6,724 were National Society Schools [44: 211]. All this was achieved before the advent of state secular schools or free or compulsory education. Yet it was not enough. Some 39 per cent of children aged between 3 and 12 were not at school: that is, one and a half million children. Nor was it a question only of unfilled places; there were one million children for whom there were no school places even had they chosen to attend [45]. The 1870 Act 'filled in the gaps'. In areas where voluntary provision was insufficient to absorb the potential children then School Boards were to be established to build nonsectarian schools. The prospect of this and the knowledge that capital grants were to cease drove the religious societies to a final spate of school building in the early 1870s. The work of the 2,000 new School Boards and the general compulsory education from 1880 finally achieved virtual mass literacy by the end of the century.

It is intriguing, as Lars Sandberg has pointed out, that although England was the richest and most industrially advanced country in the world in 1850, in spite of its advances it was educationally of the second rank [46]. Its literacy was exceeded by all the Scandinavian countries, Germany, Switzerland and Holland. Levels of human capital in the 1850s curiously related more closely to GNP rankings of the 1970s rather than to those of Victorian times. It suggests that the long-term causal linkage is from education to economic growth more than the reverse.

2 Was There a Technical Education?

The literacy education of the masses was of questionable value to industrialisation before the 1830s: it was probably more important that education and self-education had created a scientific culture among the middle classes.

This was rooted in the 1662 Act of Uniformity which led to the expulsion from their livings of 2,000 dissenting clergymen, including tutors at Oxford and Cambridge. Many became private teachers although this was not legalised until the Act of Toleration in 1689. Sons of dissenting families were likewise barred from studying at the ancient universities in England and accordingly sought out their co-religionist tutors. Thus arose the Dissenting Academies which provided an alternative form of higher education to that offered at Oxford and Cambridge [47][48]. There were 23 academies even in the illegal period 1663–90. A further 34 are traceable in the period 1690–1750 to which were added another three, including perhaps the most famous at Warrington, after 1750. Nicholas Hans found that some 150 ejected dissenting clergy opened educational establishments of some sort [49: 58].

The academies had an especial interest in science, largely for theological reasons. The study of the workings of natural law was thought to reveal the existence of rational design in the universe and hence of a Creator God. This was evident from the title of the most influential textbook used in the academies, John Ray's *Wisdom of God Manifest in the Works of Creation* (1691). Moreover, following Locke's belief that all knowledge came to the mind through the senses, their approach to science was empirical and experimental with much emphasis on practical laboratory equipment. In this way scientific truths, which were also Godly truths, could be palpably demonstrated to the senses as the means of making them acceptable to the reason [50]. Of course this linking of science with theology was not unique to Dissenters. Anglicans (like Newton) would make a similar connection and many Anglicans opened private schools as profit-making nonsectarian institutions in the eighteenth century. What was distinctive about the Dissenting Academies was the needs of their founders for alternative teaching careers as a result of their exclusion from university posts and of the similar exclusion of their clientele of co-religionist students from English universities. Some of these were training to be Nonconformist clergy. Above all many Dissenting Academies achieved standards of academic excellence.

Accordingly, many academies became highly reputable centres of scientific education. For example eight Fellows of the Royal Society taught variously at academies in Moorfields, Hoxton and Homerton in London, and in Manchester and Warrington in Lancashire. Indeed, Joseph Priestley gained his FRS for his work in the last of these. Newton was in touch with Moorfields and Hoxton, tutors from Oxford and Cambridge taught science at Newington Green in London, Shrewsbury and Sheriffhales in Shropshire and Rathmell in the West Riding of Yorkshire, while tutors of Scottish scientific education taught at Kendal, Warrington and Bethnal Green. We should bear in mind that two of the leading English scientists of the eighteenth century taught not at Oxford or Cambridge but in Lancashire in dissenting academies: Joseph Priestley (the discoverer of oxygen) at Warrington and John Dalton (a pioneer of atomic physics) at Blackburn. The academies also pioneered business education. Warrington ran a three-year course for commercial students, combining science, languages, book-keeping, geography and trade subjects. Some 98 students passed through it between 1757 and 1780 [51].

The academies were also important in diffusing a scientific culture beyond their own towns and their permanent students. They acted as bases for itinerant scientific lecturing over a wide area [52]. For example, Caleb Rotherham of Kendal Academy (who was educated at Edinburgh University and in Holland) gave lecture tours in the north-west and Robert Goodacre of Nottingham toured in South Yorkshire. Most important were itinerants, not necessarily attached to institutions, who travelled the country giving scientific lectures rather in the manner of touring actors. Such were John Warltire, the Adam Walkers (father and son), James Ferguson and others [53]. They would put up at a hotel and take a theatre to give a few weeks' lectures or provide short courses for schools like Eton and Rugby. East Anglia even had its own local circuit toured by a lecturer who combined his educational work with selling scientific instruments and spectacles [54]. Ian Inkster finds for Sheffield that the itinerants 'were fundamental in the formation of an intellectual community' [55] and so it must have been in most late eighteenth-century towns where a scientific culture flourished.

Towns seeking something of a more permanent nature than the intermittent lectures established scientific clubs which became an important part of the continuative and self-education of the cultured commercial and professional classes. There had been an early-eighteenth-century tradition of these in the east, at Spalding, Peterborough and smaller towns around the Fens. However, the first important such society in an industrial centre, and the most famous, was the Lunar Society of Birmingham which flourished from the 1760s to around 1800, with its apogee in the 1780s [56]. Here the industrialists Wedgwood and Boulton, the scientist Priestley and the Scottish scientist–businessmen, Watt, Keir and Roebuck exchanged ideas. The idea spread with the Manchester Literary and Philosophical Society, started in 1781, and the Derby Philosophical Society – an offshoot of the Lunar in 1782. Other northern towns began similar institutions and by the mid nineteenth century there were thirteen 'Lit and Phils' in Lancashire and Yorkshire, five in the West Country, three in the North East and one each in the Midlands and East Anglia [57: *134*]. In London a similar role was played by the coffee houses where scientists met, notably Rawthmell's in Covent Garden out of whose meetings grew the Royal Society of Arts for the promotion of the application of science to manufactures and commerce [58][59].

There was also a rise in scientific publishing. The Manchester Lit. and Phil. was unusual in publishing its transactions, while other journals, for example *The Philosophical Magazine* and the *Journal of Natural Philsophy* likewise flourished in 1780–1800. Middle-class scientific self-education was a strong late-Georgian fashion. The attending of lectures, reading of papers, formation of clubs and libraries among doctors, businessmen, middle-class radicals and manufacturers became a socially integrating activity much as the playing of golf was to do a century later. At comparatively minimal cost it created a well-to-do community, well disposed to science, in which industrialisation could thrive.

Finally in London the Royal Institution was founded in 1799. Growing from its initial concerns of rural philanthropy and scientific agricultural improvement it was concerned to apply science to entrepreneurial and professional purposes. Its leading scientists Sir Humphrey Davy and Michael Faraday provided popular and serious lectures, laboratory research and journal publication and involved themselves in a range of practical work from the miner's lamp to prison disinfection [60].

Optimistic as this view is it is not without its sceptics. Roy Porter considers that the industrially utilitarian aspects of provincial science have been overstressed. Its devotees he sees as gentlemen, professional men and minor gentry rather than manufacturers. They were seeking science as part of Enlightenment culture – akin to literature, the theatre, concert-going, not as the basis for or response to the needs of industrialisation [61]. Support for Porter's view is provided by a close study of Manchester College (the former Warrington Academy) from 1786. There business students attended for a year or less not for vocational studies but 'liberal conversation and polite knowledge'. When the College moved to York, 1803–40, industrialists' sons were prominent yet only 19 per cent went into business [62]. Three-quarters were being diverted into the professions, mostly into the Church. Furthermore, however fertile this seedbed was in England, it was not quite strong enough in itself to generate the scientific changes vital for the industrial revolution. These depended on an adjacent culture, that of Scottish education and science. Although this book is confined to England, yet in this instance we cannot understand the situation without some reference to north of the Border.

There were various reasons why science occupied a more important place in Scottish than in English education. Firstly, there was the prestige of medicine in the Scottish universities. In Scotland, unlike England, the doctor was a university-trained man and part of this training included chemistry. Accordingly, chemistry acquired some of the reflected prestige of the subject it served. Secondly, Scotland had close intellectual links with Holland, facilitated by geography and reinforced by a shared Calvinist Protestantism. Leiden was a major centre for both medical and chemical studies and Scottish graduates travelled there to the lectures of the great Dutch doctors and chemists Boerhaave and Gaubius, just as the late Victorians were to seek out the German professors. Thirdly, Scottish industry faced a severe chemical problem earlier and on a larger scale then England. This was that of bleaching the linen which dominated their textile trades. There were limits to what could be done with sun and rain and the ashes of birch bark and kelp used for bleach. The search for a chemical bleach, into which the universities were called was of only limited success until about 1750. Yet it gave an urgency to chemical education and research throughout the eighteenth century.

It was from the Scottish educational environment that the two most important inventions came into England: the separate condenser and bleach. As is well known, the condenser gave the fuel economy which enabled the steam engine to be used in factories and locations other than coal mines. This was devised by James Watt, instrument maker at Glasgow University where Joseph Black, whose principle of latent heat it embodied, was Professor of Natural Philosophy. The bleach problem was solved in two stages. Sulphuric acid – vitriol – was mass-produced by the lead chamber process devised by John Roebuck who, although an Englishman, was a graduate of Edinburgh University. Initially, diluted vitriol was used as a bleach in itself. Then, when the French Leblanc process solved the problem of turning salt into soda for bleach, vitriol was also necessary for this process. Without the condenser and the vitriol for soda-making the English cotton industry would have been stifled. Both were the products of Scottish scientists and technologists from Scottish universities, and to that degree was English industry beholden to the Scottish education system [63]. In a direct way, too, scientifically-educated Scottish migrant entrepreneurs, scientists and educators enriched English industrial life: Watt, Roebuck and Keir in Birmingham, and Rotherham, the proprietor of Kendal Academy, among others. Reciprocally, the Scottish universities proved highly popular with English dissenters who sought a higher education there. Through them the lectures of Cullen and Black further enhanced the general scientific culture of England.

(ii) THE MECHANICS' INSTITUTES

The developments described so far chiefly affected the comfortably-off business and professional classes. But in the 1820s there was an attempt to create a scientific culture and technical education for the working classes also. This too came initially from Scotland. George Birkbeck, a doctor in Glasgow, used to give scientific lectures to working men at the institution created by former Glasgow professor, John Anderson, in 1796 (now the University of Strathclyde) [64]. On settling in London, Birkbeck was instrumental, with Benthamite radicals, in the formation of the London Mechanics' Institute in 1823. The idea was to provide tuition in physics and chemistry for artificers, mechanics and craftsmen of various kinds. This was not only important in its own right but also became the model for a provincial movement [65]. Henry Brougham toured the country urging towns to establish similar institutions and they spread, especially in the north of England [66]. Numerically their spread was impressive. There were 100 such institutes by 1826 and over 300 by 1841. In some cities, initially at least, they tried to serve a serious scientific educative purpose. It was so in London, Liverpool, Manchester, and Leeds where local businessmen Gott and Marshall were strongly in favour of scientific education [67]. However, things began to go wrong. Birkbeck had doubted whether the literacy level in England was high enough to support further education of some scientific rigour. His doubts proved well founded. Accordingly most of the institutes took different paths in response to various other social pressures. Since it was impossible to give scientific lectures to illiterate men many institutes concentrated on basic education in reading and writing instead (e.g. Ancoats, Bolton). Others became social clubs for recreation and foreshadowed the working men's club movement of the 1860s. Others again became centres of radical political activity (e.g. Cheltenham), Chartist, Co-operative, trade unionist or any other in the kaleidoscope of interests which sought the working man's attention in the 1830s and 1840s. Conversely some institutes forgot their origins and were taken over by the middle classes either as cultural centres for themselves (in Sheffield 88 per cent of members were business or professional men), or as institutions in which an attempt could be made to persuade the working classes of the virtues of temperance (e.g. Rotherham) or classical political economy (e.g. Leeds). It became almost surprising to find some (e.g. Falmouth) which retained both a scientific purpose and a working-class membership.

Two things are clear about this movement. Firstly, the institutes were not an entire failure. They fulfilled a variety of useful roles relevant to their time and locality and whatever path of divergence away from the original intention that was taken by each institution depended purely on local circumstances. Royle suggests that 'the mechanics institutes contributed to the intellectual – and thereby political – emancipation of working men' [68: *318*], while Inkster sees them as 'part of a profound, provincial based middle class culture' [69: *204*]. Secondly, the negative point is equally unavoidable. Whatever Birkbeck and Brougham had hoped, the mechanics institutes did not prove to be a mass movement giving working men that scientific culture which the middle classes had enjoyed since the mid eighteenth century.

(iii) SOUTH KENSINGTON AND AFTER

In the mid-century the state became involved in the promotion of technical education in national institutions focused in London [70]. In 1845 the Royal College of Chemistry was established partly on the initiative of the Prince Consort. It was intended as a means of introducing German organic chemistry into England, and its first principal, A. W. Hofmann, was nominated by Liebig himself. Following this the Government School of Mines was created in 1851. Both these institutions benefited from the Great Exhibition of 1851 whose profits of £186,000, together with a Government grant, purchased the site in South Kensington where it was intended to gather various scientific institutions. In 1853 the School of Mines (in Jermyn Street) incorporated the nationalised College of Chemistry (in Oxford Street), the latter transferring to South Kensington in 1872 and the former joining it piecemeal thereafter. The value of the Royal College of Chemistry was considerable. It was there in 1856 that W. H. Perkin's research discovered the first aniline dye, mauve. Its more routine output of students went in large numbers to steel, dye, sugar and other works requiring chemists, especially organic chemists of which the College was a rare provider in England.

In 1853 the Government took another initiative in creating the Department of Science and Art which controlled the School and the College. It also tried to create science schools in the provinces, though with limited success. Most importantly, in 1859 the new Department began a series of science examinations for schools and other institutions wishing to present pupils. The Department paid grants to such schools for successful pupils on a payment by results basis. In 1860 there were nine schools with 500 pupils participating in the scheme. By 1870 this had risen to 799 schools with 34,283 pupils [71]. It represented a considerable effort to introduce science teaching into schools, its standards secured by the financial control of government inspectors.

Notwithstanding the developments of the 1850s and 1860s the limitations of English scientific and technical education by the end of the 1860s had become evident at the Paris Exhibition of 1867. This was a major turning point. Whereas Britain had won most of the prizes at the Exhibition of 1851 our performance at Paris was poor. There was a strong feeling that we had fallen behind the French and the Prussians and this prompted renewed concern about technical education at home. Immediately the Nussey brothers, who had written a report on woollen textiles at the Exhibition, returned to Leeds to start the movement for a Yorkshire College of Science (the future University of Leeds) to enable the West Riding to match the French. Thus, the national unease generated helped to initiate the civic universities movement of the 1870s and 1880s. It also found immediate expression in the setting up of the 1868 Parliamentary Select Committee on scientific education chaired by the ironmaster Bernhard Samuelson. This began nearly 20 years of various parliamentary investigations into science, industry and education which led to improvements in technical education, especially after 1890.

Two main points suggest themselves so far. Firstly, the industrial revolution in England seemed inadvertently to have struck an economically efficient balance in its provision of education whatever its social deficiencies. It was a balance struck not by any conscious central or governmental planning but by a cumulation of individual private decisions determining the withholding or directing of expenditure. Little serious attempt was made before the 1830s to maintain the elementary education of the mass of the population whose literacy in the industrial areas was allowed to decline. This had no adverse economic effects since most of the new occupations being created by the new industrialisation did not in any case require literate labour. Indeed, to have undertaken the investment necessary to sustain literacy levels in the later decades of the eighteenth century and beginning of the nineteenth might have required a serious diversion of resources away from the industrialisation itself. For example, an Arkwright water frame mill and a National school were roughly comparable in cost. After 1840 England was sufficiently rich to be able to finance expensive projects like its railway building and the considerable expansion of investment in education. But this was not so in the 1780–1810 period when the money was more efficiently and desirably spent on the industrial plant, canals and military expenditure that characterised these years. By contrast, the creation of a middle-class scientific subculture was cheap, paid for by the participants and limited to relatively few people. This modest expenditure on higher levels of education and self-education was arguably more appropriate for industrialisation (at least in the short term) than any attempt to sustain 60 per cent male literacy rates in Lancashire. The industrial revolution in England did not thrive because all the education supporting it was ample and valuable. It derived part of its strength from the employment of scarce resources in the areas of greatest urgency – the industrial investment and a cheaply-created middle-class scientific culture. In the event this strength was not sapped by the diversion of funds into a potentially very expensive attempt to sustain elementary education. If there were short-term gains for industrialisation arising from the neglect of elementary education for the masses, the long-term effects were more questionable. It confirmed England as a country (unlike Scotland, France and Prussia of the time) where education was not seen as a right and it established low levels of expectation in terms of both what the working classes received and what they came to regard as appropriate for themselves.

Secondly, if this expenditure was postponed, so too was a problem. While scientific and technical information circulated well in middle-class institutions, the attempt to create a technical education for working men was a failure, whatever other worthy purposes the mechanics' institutes served. Apart from the central institutions in South Kensington and the quite successful attempt by the Department of Science and Art to introduce technical examinations into schools in the 1860s (as we have seen) these years of the nineteenth century spanned a dangerous flagging in the provision of technical education. This was all the more dangerous in that it was from the 1820s that the German states were developing their Technical High Schools and various forms of continuative education, all resting on high mass literacy stemming from the educational reforms following the 1806 defeat at Jena. The roots of a great deal of English anxiety about the level of education *vis-à-vis*

Germany in the 1870s and 1880s lay in the lack of development in the 1850s and 1860s. Industrial success bred a lack of urgency to make rising literacy the basis for a higher level of working-class scientific training – as Brougham and Birkbeck had wanted a generation earlier. Accordingly, the lively middle-class scientific culture of the eighteenth century was not transmitted down the social scale until much later in the nineteenth century with adverse effects for British industry hardly felt before 1867.

3 A 'Middle-Class' Education

(i) THE PRIVATE SCHOOLS, GRAMMAR SCHOOLS AND SOCIAL CHANGE

In the early decades of the nineteenth century public attention had been chiefly focused on the elementary education of the lower orders. Yet important changes were also taking place in private middle- and upper-class education. In the eighteenth century, families who aimed to raise their sons as gentlemen and who could afford to do so employed tutors to educate their children at home. Home education was thought to be more conducive to virtue than the public schools with their low moral state and harsh corporal punishment. Indeed, most educational theory in the eighteenth century was expressed in terms of a domestic tutor–pupil context.

The rising urban population and living standards brought an increase in middle-class families able to afford modest fees for private day schooling in their home towns. Accordingly many such academies or proprietorial schools began to be advertised in the later decades of the eighteenth century. J. H. Plumb finds a rapid increase in such schools for the commercial classes especially after 1770 and finds 91 advertised in Ipswich alone between 1783 and 1787 [72: 73]. This is confirmed by evidence from Cheshire which shows a sharp rise in private schools advertised from 6 in the 1750s and 1760s, to 41 in the 1780s and 1790s [4: 173–6]. Leicestershire evidence also suggests that this rapid growth continued into the early decades of the nineteenth century [73]. These middle-class demands for education, notably in the towns, were similarly to revitalise the grammar schools and subsequently the public boarding schools.

The grammar schools responded strongly to demands for middle-class education. Their origins can be traced to Colet's statutes for St Paul's in 1518 which provided for humanist studies in Greek as well as Latin. The creation of the Tudor grammar schools followed in this mould. By the eighteenth century, however, it was unclear what 'grammar school' meant. Many taught elementary subjects sometimes with classics, took all social classes, included girls and acted simply as the local village or parochial school. Two pressures forced change and polarisation on the schools. The inflation from the 1760s to 1815 obliged schools which could not match it with rising endowment funds to seek additional sources of income. The rise of a prosperous urban commercial class provided them with a clientele from which to draw this income.

Three things began to happen as a process of adjustment.

Firstly, grammar schools began to change their curricula, often including commercial subjects either instead of or alongside classics [74]. In a sample of 334 eighteenth-century grammar schools, R. S. Tompson finds relatively few incidences of change, only in 41 schools between 1700 and 1750. But by the last decades such changes were common and rapid, in 21 schools in the 1770s, in 28 in the 1780s and in 29 in the 1790s, as the grammar schools competed with the curricula of the growing private schools. Secondly, the new curricula enabled the schools to charge fees. Whereas only 36 of Tompson's sample of 334 charged fees before 1750, 223 (two-thirds) did so by 1837. There was a decisive shift to a fee-paying middle-class clientele and away from the poorer former free pupils. This was also facilitated by Lord Eldon's judgement in the Leeds Grammar School case of 1805 which decided that grammar schools should not use their endowments to teach non-classical subjects free of charge. The lower orders did not want classics and they could no longer benefit from receiving a free elementary education at the grammar school. Thirdly, some schools pressed further along this road and turned themselves into boarding schools – Victorian public schools in embryo. By 1837, 138 of Tompson's sample had done so, most between 1800 and 1837. In short, after about 1780 grammar schools, from being charitable institutions teaching elementary subjects and classics to boys and girls of all social classes, were increasingly becoming middle-class fee-paying institutions dealing with secondary education. Now they also included commercial subjects for business as well as classics for university entrance.

In the mid nineteenth century, three factors revitalised even those grammar schools that had already made the change and reformed those which had not. Firstly, a new breed of headmaster seemed to appear at this time, of high Victorian moral purpose and strength of personality. Such men often took over ailing or mediocre grammar schools and made them centres of academic endeavour; they included Caldicott at Bristol (1860), Jessop at Norwich (1859), Rigaud and Holden at Ipswich (1851, 1858), Mitchinson at Canterbury (1859). and Walker at Manchester (1859). Secondly, the schools were stimulated by the creation of a system of 'middle-class' examinations from the 1850s [75]. These had been started as a private venture in Exeter by T. D. Acland in 1856. So great was the demand for them that their administration was taken over by Oxford and Cambridge in 1858 and they became known as the Local examinations. Schools of the highest quality tended not to use them for their best pupils whom they still directed towards university entrance examinations. But for middle-class boys not intending to go to university they were a valuable school-leaving qualification and they gave grammar schools something to aim for, and a perception of how successfully they measured up to a common standard. The Higher Locals began at Cambridge in 1869 and at Oxford in 1877. In 1873 the Oxford and Cambridge Schools Examining Board was set up. All these were the origins of the present 'GCSE' and 'A' level examinations, the incentives to endeavour and guarantees of standards both then and now.

The third factor revitalising the grammar schools was the Taunton Commission which investigated some 800 endowed schools between 1864 and 1867. It addressed the problem of middle-class parents in many towns who could not afford to send children to public boarding schools but who desired a local grammar school offering a curriculum which would provide their sons with an entry to the universities and the professions [76]. There remained many towns where such schools did not exist in spite of the process of social change described by Tompson and the work of Chancery in reforming individual schools in the 1860s. The Taunton Commission saw the solution as the abolition of free education in grammar schools. This would exclude free boys from the lower middle-class artisan and tradesman classes who had no university or professional ambitions and enable the curriculum to be determined by the market demand of fee-payers. This would also save the study of classics which was required of university entrants. Accordingly, one intention of the founders (free education) was thus to be sacrificed to secure the other (an academic curriculum including classics). The local grammar school was to be remodelled on the pattern of the reforming public schools. The Endowed Schools Act of 1869 established three Commissioners who, by making schemes and regulations for some 3,000 endowments, created throughout the country the middle-class fee-paying academic grammar school. Their defect was in failing to provide for the tradesman–artisan class who had to resort to the new Board Schools created after 1870.

(ii) THE RISE OF THE PUBLIC SCHOOLS

At a higher level than the grammar schools were the public boarding schools, one of the most successful and dynamic areas of the educational system at this time [77]. The body of Victorian public schools was made up of various groups. There were the ancient nine schools investigated by the Clarendon Commission in the 1860s (Eton, Winchester, Harrow, Charterhouse, Rugby, Westminster, Merchant Taylors, St Paul's and Shrewsbury). To these were added certain grammar schools changing their status like Sedburgh and Giggleswick. There were also waves of totally new foundations, nine in the 1840s (e.g. Rossall, Marlborough and Cheltenham) and ten in the 1860s (e.g. Clifton and Malvern). Most were proprietorial schools run as commercial ventures. Some had wider purposes; Canon Woodard's schools (e.g. Lancing and Hurstpierpoint) to promote High Anglicanism; J. L. Brereton's (e.g. Cranleigh and Framlingham) as county schools stressing science and agriculture for farmers' sons [78]. The schools achieved a cohesion informally by inter-school games playing and formally by membership of the Headmasters' Conference which met first in 1869 initially comprising the non-Clarendon public schools.

Various factors lay behind the new vitality of the public schools. Firstly, there was a decline in domestic education around 1830–50. [79]. This was because of the increasing numbers of middle-class children surviving infancy who could no longer conveniently be kept at home for tuition. They had to be sent away. Secondly, the improvement of transport facilities, both the fast road-coaches and then the railway, made possible a national market in education. Newly-founded schools or old town grammar schools could set out to attract a regional or even national catchment of clients who would reside as boarders. Thirdly, many more families began to live abroad, pursuing careers in the army, colonial service or overseas trade. For cultural and climatic reasons they preferred their children

41

to be educated in England in institutions which provided a home environment. Fourthly, the public schools were sought by newly prospering social groups who wished to confirm their status by assimilation with existing landed and professional élites. Finally, Thomas Arnold's reform of Rugby and the spread of his masters into other schools raised the whole moral tone of public schools and made them attractive to those who cared for their children's nurture and who had shunned the violence and neglect of welfare that characterised so many pre-Arnoldian public schools [80].

Important changes took place in the content of education in the public schools in this period. Most importantly the schools accepted science into their curricula, especially in the 1860s. The schools had hitherto been resistant to such developments – there were no graduate schoolmasters in science from Oxford or Cambridge and no textbooks. Various factors changed the situation. The introduction of science degrees at the ancient universities in the 1850s produced a first generation of science masters equal in social and academic standing to the classicists who dominated the public schools. Army reforms in the 1850s placed an emphasis on competitive examinations; the Sandhurst entrance examination now required two science subjects. Since commissioned service in the armed forces was a prestigious career for public school boys the schools had to adjust to prepare them for it. Most importantly the Clarendon Commission found the public schools' neglect of science a 'great practical evil' and the resulting Public Schools Act of 1868 enjoined science teaching on the schools [81].

A new generation of headmasters also came to have a personal interest in science which they encouraged in their schools: H. M. Butler and F. W. Farrer at Harrow, Frederick Temple at Rugby, George Ridding at Winchester and John Percival at Clifton. Similarly, specialist graduate science masters arose, notably J. M. Wilson who from 1859 developed Rugby as the pre-eminent scientific public school and whose views and activities had a strong influence on the Clarendon Commission. The schools were aided by science textbooks, notably those which were commissioned and published by Alexander Macmillan in the early 1870s.

Almost as important as change in the formal curriculum was a change in the value systems of the public schools. The Arnoldian ideal which had raised the tone of the schools from the 1820s was one of 'godliness and good learning'. Thomas Arnold's aim had been to produce the Christian Gentleman, the scholarly boy with a pious conscience. From the mid-century these ideals came to be replaced by a more secular and robust emphasis on manliness and character training [82]. This was expressed in a concern from the 1860s for organised games, athleticism and militarism. The 1860s saw games firmly established in the schools with inter-school competitions and the codification of standard rules. In particular the ideal of 'muscular Christianity' advocated by Thomas Hughes, Charles Kingsley and others equated virile good health with Christian values of manliness and fortitude. Games aimed to revive a slack school (as Cotton had done at Marlborough) and were also expected to counter effeminacy and engender qualities of service to the team, personal courage and patriotism [83]. Closely linked with this was the contemporary concern with militarism [84]. In a climate of political mistrust of France, official sponsorship was given to the Volunteer Rifle Club movement from 1859. Lord Elcho initiated a movement for the introduction of military drill into public schools in 1860 and the same year saw the starting of National Rifle Association competitions. Many schools began cadet corps in the 1860s, notably Eton, Winchester, Harrow and Rugby. Many more began rifle clubs or employed ex-sergeants for drill as part of physical training. As Arnold had effected a change in the ethos of the schools by emphasising piety, so a further change around the 1860s matched the public schools with secular needs outside. They aimed to produce the physically fit, patriotic and basically honourable young men with leadership qualities necessary for the Army, the Empire and the City, on which the strength of Britain depended.

These changes made the schools highly attractive to social groups of parents somewhat below the traditional clientele and there was a marked change in the social intake of such schools around the mid-century. Bamford has analysed the social class of parents at eight leading public schools for the period 1800–50. The gentry provided 38.1 per cent of boys, titled persons 12.2, clergy 12.0, professional parents 5.2 with the rest unknown or insignificant. There was an expected and large predominance of the rural élites of gentry, titled and clerical families [85]. However in the mid-century there is clear evidence of the rise of business families beginning to send their sons to Winchester, among the most distinguished of the schools. Bishop and Wilkinson find that sons of fathers in business and engineering at Winchester rose from 2.9 per cent (boys born in the 1820s and entering school in the 1830s and 1840s) to 7.4 per cent (boys born in the 1850s and entering school in the 1860s and 1870s) (86: *104–5*]. In this period grandsons of a number of the pioneers of the industrial revolution began to be sent to public schools – Mathew Boulton's and Richard Arkwright's to Eton and John Marshall's to Rugby – the third generation of monied men reinforcing their status through education [87]. As many public schools instituted entrance examinations in the 1850s this gave rise to a new sector of preparatory schools to prepare for them [88]. The expenses of getting to and going to a public school were accordingly increased and this gave a further advantage to families enriched by industrial wealth.

As more businessmen's sons went to the public schools, so in turn more public school boys chose business and industry as a career. At Winchester this rose from 7.2 per cent (boys born in the 1820s and entering careers around the 1840s) to 17.6 per cent (boys born in the 1850s and entering careers around the 1870s) [86: *64–6*]. The clergy and the law still remained the favoured professions entered by Wykehamists but this sharp increase in those choosing business and industry is striking and parallels changes in the social origins of the boys at the school. The trend is also evident elsewhere. At Marlborough those entering business rose from 6 per cent in 1846 to 17 per cent by 1866 and at Merchant Taylors from 6 per cent in 1851 to 13 per cent by 1871 [89]. Bamford likewise finds that the proportion of boys at Eton and Harrow entering business, science and engineering rose from 5.9 per cent of those whose occupations were known (boys entering school 1830 and entering careers 1840s) to 10.6 per cent (boys entering school 1860 and entering careers 1870s) [77]. Reciprocally public schoolboys came to dominate certain business professions. Whereas only 10 per cent of bankers were public schoolboys in the period 1800–20 this had risen to 62 per cent by 1861–80 [90].

These upward trends in businessmen sending their sons to public schools and in public schoolboys entering business were to be of great importance. Coleman sees the linkage of class, public school education and business leadership in the larger companies as dating from the 1860s [87]. The extended club of the public school network was to replace the older Nonconformist network that had characterised industrial revolution entrepreneurs. In turn it was to exacerbate class differences in English industrial relations. This closer engagement of the public school and business has not been regarded as a mixed blessing. It has been argued that they merely brought into business the 'gentrified' ideals of the schools 'suspicious of change, reluctant to innovate, energetic only in maintaining the status quo', and contributed to the long-term decline of the economy [91].

The strong expansion of middle-class education both in grammar and in public schools after 1830 was a response to the demands for education from parents. But in spite of the increasing rapprochement with business, this expansion was not matched by commensurate employment opportunities. Indeed it has been argued that 'the educational expansion took place in spite of a lack of suitable professional openings, not in response to the growth of new fields of employment' [77: 99]. Too many public schoolboys were being produced at a time when there were only very slowly growing opportunities in the Church, law and medicine between 1851 and 1871. Young men with middle-class aspirations outstripped the availability of careers that would give them fulfilment. The fastest growing occupations lay in lower middle-class employments like clerks and shop assistants to which ex-public schoolboys would be unlikely to be attracted. The Empire was to provide a safety valve as products of these new schools sought in the colonies lifestyles and status they could not have enjoyed at home.

4 The Universities

THESE were not glorious years for the universities. For most of the period Oxford and Cambridge reposed in a social and curricular inertia that limited their value to society. These limitations arose partly from a network of institutional arrangements and partly from assumptions arising from the concept of liberal education.

(a) *The System*

From 1780 there had been moves to raise both ancient universities from the slough into which they had sunk during the eighteenth century. In 1780 Cambridge began its Senate House written examination chiefly in mathematics and in 1800 Oxford, which had been only half full throughout the eighteenth century [93], began its Public Examination mainly in classics with some mathematics. Some diversification came at Oxford in 1807 with the creation of the School of Mathematics and Physics and at Cambridge in 1824 when the Classical Tripos was instituted to join the prestigious Mathematical Tripos. These changes created an examination structure providing the serious student with the incentive to exertion. But they also had the effect of concentrating the curriculum narrowly on classics at Oxford and mathematics at Cambridge. Subjects outside the examination structure, notably science at Oxford, accordingly declined. Moreover this narrowness was compounded by a complex of social and organisational factors.

In particular the social class of intake into both Oxford and Cambridge was remarkably narrow and stable throughout this period. Anderson and Schnaper found that between 1752 and 1886 51.4 per cent of Oxford students and 58.1 per cent of those at Cambridge came from two social groups, the gentry and the clergy. Indeed 90.4 per cent of Oxford students came from gentry, clergy or military backgrounds and there was no conspicuous alteration over the whole period [94: 6]. Another study found that 69 per cent of Cambridge students came from landowning and clergy families in the period 1752–99 and 63 per cent in the period 1800–49 [93]. The future careers of graduates was even narrower, 64 per cent of Oxford and 54 per cent of Cambridge men going into the Church between 1752 and 1886 [94: 6].

The student body was limited by the close connection of the ancient universities with the Church of England. The requirement that matriculants at Oxford and graduates at Cambridge should subscribe to the Thirty-Nine Articles excluded Nonconformists. The universities were thus isolated from the new potential clientele of Nonconformist business families enriched by the industrial revolution. Hence the heavy weighting of landed gentry and clergy families in their intake. The intake was also socially limited by the expense of a course which could cost over £300 a year. As a result of the high costs Oxford became socially very exclusive in the second quarter of the nineteenth century, when admissions also stagnated after an expansion following the Napoleonic Wars [93]. Because of the high cost of education many men needed to win scholarships, the bulk of which were in classics and mathematics. The scholarships had been endowed over the centuries and inevitably related to the subjects then dominant and not to those – notably science – required in the nineteenth century. Since boys needed scholarships and since these were only offered in the older subjects, the schools focused their teaching on them and this was a further element perpetuating a classical curriculum in the grammar schools and in the universities.

The provision of fellowships also had a similar effect. The ablest men at Oxford had studied classics at school, won classical scholarships and accordingly they in turn became the best undergraduates and so the most eligible for teaching fellowships at the end of their student careers. Most fellowships were tied to classics at Oxford and mathematics at Cambridge. Those that were discretionary and not so tied tended to be filled by classicists and mathematicians since they were the most able graduates available and these were the subjects required for teaching the next generation of undergraduates. In this way the whole financial scholarship–fellowship system locked the older subjects onto the ancient universities.

This was also tied in with two power struggles. The most important of these was between the colleges and the universities. At

Oxford and Cambridge the colleges were powerful and wealthy and the universities relatively weak as financial and administrative entities. This suited the colleges who ran themselves like private companies with the fellows sharing out the profits at the end of the year audit. The colleges were well aware that classics and mathematics were very cheap subjects to teach, and they did not entail research or expensive equipment or even rapidly growing libraries. Thus there were very strong financial grounds for the fellows of colleges wishing to continue teaching what they knew and which caused them least trouble. They also had a vested interest in the low cost of the subjects which would not entail the colleges in fresh expenditure which in turn would reduce their profits and personal incomes. The colleges were not only conservative about curriculum for financial reasons, they also feared a tilting of the balance of power in favour of the universities. They saw clearly that if science or engineering were introduced then this would require laboratory building on a greater scale than they could manage for themselves. It would entail each university having to create its own buildings, resulting in the respective universities becoming increasingly powerful *vis-à-vis* the colleges. Moreover, since the universities had very little money of their own, the funds necessary to enable them to embark on such projects would have to be raised by taxing the college revenues. More university power would also diminish college autonomy. Thus curricular conservatism was rooted in the defence of a private financial system and resistance to the growth of centralised power in the university.

This in turn was linked with an important argument from the 1860s about research as a function of the university [96]. Advocates of research, dons like Mark Pattison and Henry Halford Vaughan, were influenced by German universities which accepted the discovery of new knowledge as part of their obligations. They wished to move Oxford and Cambridge away from being merely advanced public schools, teaching a relatively static curriculum and feeling no duty to extend existing subjects or to develop new ones by research. The research party advocated a strong professoriat, and university laboratories and libraries on German lines expending more money on research in the sciences, history, archaeology and so forth. At Cambridge, likewise, Sheldon Rothblatt has detected a new seriousness of purpose among the dons from the 1860s; 'They were distinguished by their professional interest in scholarship', and by a rejection of 'donnish' self-indulgent idleness that had characterised too many of their predecessors [97: 227].

The arts versus science argument was thus inextricably involved with a set of institutional arrangements deriving from the financial provision of scholarships and fellowships, the clash of the colleges and their universities, the fellows versus the professoriat and the teachers versus the researchers. Until some hammer could be taken to the autonomy of the colleges, the curricular conservatism rooted in college-based anti-research teaching would be perpetuated in the older universities. They in turn would continue to exert the curricular stranglehold over the schools which aimed to send their boys to Oxford and Cambridge.

(b) *The Liberal Education Debate*

There was another dimension to this situation, since curricular conservatism was defended as a positive virtue in the lively debate about liberal education which spanned these years [98][99]. In 1809 R. L. Edgeworth published his *Essays on Professional Education* in which, in an attack on contemporary university studies, he roundly stated that 'the value of all education must ultimately be decided by its utility'. The book was immediately taken up with approval by the *Edinburgh Review*, the organ of radical Benthamite utilitarian interests, and in that journal the Reverend Sydney Smith, a former Oxford fellow, used his review of Edgeworth's book to attack his old university. Classics, according to both Edgeworth and Smith, was patently a useless form of study.

Their viewpoint, so crudely utilitarian in both senses, at once stung Oxford and called forth an early attempt to defend classical studies. This was the *Reply to the Calumnies of the Edinburgh Review* published in 1810 by Edward Copleston, the Provost of Oriel College, Oxford. Copleston's argument contained two essential propositions. Firstly, he made a distinction between ends and means, arguing that some activities and qualities are ends in themselves and not to be justified by reference to some end beyond themselves. The high sense of honour and love of glory associated with the classics were good in themselves. Secondly, Copleston argued that as well as being an 'end in itself' the study of classics by fitting a man for no particular occupation thereby fitted him for all of them. This was a belief which was to become very influential in the mid-century when the general intellectual training given by classics was regarded as the most suitable for civil service recruitment through public examinations.

Copleston was defending classics, but in the 1830s William Whewell, the Master of Trinity, made a similar defence of Cambridge mathematics as the basis of liberal education [100]. For him there was a crucial distinction between truths that were merely empirical – laws based on the observation of recurring phenomena (e.g. that buttercups are yellow) – and truths that were *necessarily* and inevitably true (e.g. Pythagoras' theorem on the properties of a triangle). Only mathematics dealt with these necessary and inevitable truths and it was accordingly superior as a vehicle for education to any other. In particular it was superior to philosophy which dwelt too much on opinion and uncertainty.

The culmination of the old liberal education ideal was expressed by John Henry Newman in his famous *Discourses on University Education* which he gave in Dublin in 1852 [101]. Newman was an ex-fellow of Oriel College and steeped in Oxford assumptions about classics and liberal education. For him, as for Copleston, liberal education was that which 'stands on its own pretensions, which is independent of sequel' and did not need to be justified by a utility beyond itself. Liberal education made the gentleman, it was 'the especial characteristic or property of a University and of a gentleman'. The end result of such education was 'a cultivated intellect, a delicate taste, a candid equitable dispassionate mind'. The purpose, accordingly, was not vocational training in any particular skill but the general development of the intellect and of moral and social qualities for their own sake. As a secondary consideration, a man so educated could 'fill any post with credit and master any subject with facility'. John Stuart Mill, a non-university man who rather disliked universities, held similar views. Their purpose was to create 'capable and cultivated human beings', not to provide professional instruction for specific vocations [102]. Liberal education sought to develop both 'broad liberal sympathies' and a creative flexible intelligence on the one hand, but also a mind rigorously disciplined to precision through the study of subjects 'uncongenial, unpleasant and downright difficult'. Such education was supposed to be both generously widening and sharply refining to the developing mind [103].

This expressed what the ancient universities thought about themselves and what many others outside conceived the purpose of university education to be. They helped to bolster the curricular conservatism of Oxford and Cambridge based on classics and mathematics. In the provinces these attitudes had a more dangerous effect in over-influencing some new institutions to follow the traditions of the older universities rather than to develop more appropriate directions of their own.

(c) *Reform*

From the mid-century the ancient universities began a limited reform [104][105]. Following Royal Commissions for both universities in 1852, an Act for Oxford in 1854 and for Cambridge in 1856 enabled Nonconformists both to matriculate and to graduate. This, while solving one problem, created another as graduated dissenters were still barred from becoming fellows of colleges throughout the 1860s. These disabilities were finally removed by the Universities' Religious Tests Act of 1871 which also obviated the need for fellows to be ordained clergymen. In the period 1813–30 92 per cent of Oxford dons were ordained clergymen and 40 per cent of them were to take up full-time ecclesiastical careers usually after 10 or 15 years as a university teacher. The 1871 Act was an important landmark in the transition from clergyman to don and the emergence of a secular academic profession in Victorian England [107]. They had, however, to remain bachelors until the reform of college statutes in the 1870s and 1880s. In the 1850s following the Acts of 1854 and 1856 colleges at Oxford and Cambridge reformed their scholarship systems by removing closed privileges still enjoyed by the descendants and remote relations of benefactors.

There was also some curricular innovation. Cambridge in 1848 established two new triposes in Natural Sciences and Moral Sciences which included history and law. In 1850 Oxford established its Schools of Law and Modern History and of Natural Science. Initially at Oxford these could only be taken after 'Greats' (the Literae Humaniores classics degree) but from 1866 could be taken as specialised subjects in themselves. Since both universities now claimed to teach science to degree level they both built laboratories, the Oxford Museum in 1855 and the New Museum at Cambridge from 1865. Indeed Oxford, in contrast to its later record was receptive to science in the 1850s and 1860s and especially good in chemistry, anatomy and physiology [108]. However, we need not exaggerate the impact of this. For example, before 1860 no more than 10 students a year took the Natural Sciences Tripos at Cambridge and before 1870 no more than 20 a year. Most wranglers (first class mathematicians) at Cambridge in the early nineteenth century became teachers or clergymen [109].

The watershed for Oxford and Cambridge came after 1870 with the Cleveland Commission of 1873 leading to the Act of 1877 and in turn to Commissioners to revise the statutes of colleges. The latter were obliged to release some of their funds for the creation of scientific professorships and university institutions. Only then, with this rebalancing of power between the colleges and the universities was it possible to create an Oxford and Cambridge more oriented to research in science and scholarship, professional training, a widening curriculum and a strong professoriat with well-endowed university laboratory and library provision. But in 1870 much of this lay in the future.

(ii) PROVINCIAL REFLECTIONS

In spite of the defects of Oxford and Cambridge there was no effective civic universities movement which could serve as an alternative before 1870. Durham University had been founded in 1832 by the Church of England, partly to allay criticism of its idle wealth and chiefly to provide a higher education for potential clergymen in the north. It became virtually a clergy training college with 90 per cent of its students going into Holy Orders. Yet by trying to ape Oxford without having the latter's resources it had very little success with poor students. This in turn diminished its credibility in the eyes of local industrialists who rejected it in favour of Newcastle as a centre of urgently needed mining education.

Owens College, Manchester, fared little better. It began in 1851 with £100,000 left by John Owens, a local textile manufacturer. Yet his intention was not a technological university to serve industry but a college to give 'instruction in the branches of learning and science usually taught in the English universities', i.e. the traditional curriculum of Oxford and Cambridge. The first principal, A. J.

Scott, compounded this by giving an introductory address reiterating some themes of Newman's recent addresses on liberal education. The Manchester business classes were not interested in a pale imitation of Oxford languishing in Richard Cobden's old house in Quay Street. It was not until the 1870s when it acquired a new sense of purpose in service to industry, a new site and ample funds that Manchester began to take its place in the forefront of the civic universities movement [110][111]. Both Durham and Owens before 1870 were abortive provincial initiatives stifled by the ancient universities and misguided into the dead end of being deferential and unsuccessful imitations rather than challenging alternatives.

A more vital root of the future civic universities movement in these years was the emergence of provincial medical schools [112]. The Apothecaries' Act of 1815 made it illegal to practise as an apothecary unless licensed by the Society of Apothecaries. This stimulated the creation of medical schools preparing students for the Apothecaries' examinations and, from 1831, those of the Royal College of Surgeons. Accordingly such schools began in Manchester (1825), Sheffield (1827), Birmingham (1828), Bristol (1828), Leeds (1830), Liverpool (1834) and Newcastle (1834). They provided one of the strands out of which civic universities were to be created in these cities after 1870, usually by the merger of some science or technical school with a pre-existing medical school formed in the 1820s and 1830s.

(iii) A RADICAL ALTERNATIVE

By contrast with Durham and Owens, the origins of the University of London were rooted in frank antipathy to the ancient universities and not in any concern to reproduce them [113]. Its prime movers were admirers of universities in Scotland, post-Napoleonic Prussia and Virginia. Many, notably Brougham and Hume, were followers of Jeremy Bentham. Accordingly, the new institution which opened in 1828 sharply differed from the existing English tradition in three main respects. Firstly, it was to be free of religious tests and open to dissenters and unbelievers. Indeed many of the early supporters were radical atheists who detested religion in general and the privileged position of the Anglican Established Church in particular. Secondly, it was to be cheaper than the ancient universities and to cater for 'middling rich people'. Thirdly and most important, there was a strong emphasis on professional training in the medical, legal, engineering and economic studies neglected at Oxford and Cambridge. It was to be useful and vocational following Bentham's belief in a utilitarian education. The Church did not regard with equanimity the creation of the new college in 'Godless Gower Street', as it was known by its sobriquet, haunt of radicals, atheists and Scotsmen. Accordingly it established its own rival King's College in 1828 as a specifically Anglican institution but following its predecessor's emphasis on professional training. From 1828 the University of London had been what is now University College. From 1836 the University of London became the body managing the examinations and degrees for its now constituent colleges, University and King's. From 1858 it became an examining body dealing not only with London institutions but providing external examinations for all comers. This was to be a vital root of the civic universities movement after 1870, since it gave a uniformity of standards for which fledgling provincial colleges could aim in their growth to maturity. In the meantime it was London rather than the provinces which between 1830 and 1870 provided the necessary alternative higher education to that provided by Oxford and Cambridge.

The chief criticism levelled at the universities in this period is that by their neglect of science they contributed so little to the needs of industrialisation. The Devonshire Commission reporting in the 1870s still found Oxford and Cambridge sciences of 'inadequate amount' [106]. The role of Oxford and Cambridge was essentially to produce clergy, gentlemen and, from the 1850s, civil servants. They did not appeal to the commercial classes or to the new professions like the engineers [114]. Nor did Durham or Manchester before 1870; only the London colleges thrived on a close linkage with the new business and professional classes.

The university sector as a whole did not keep pace with rising population. In the early eighteenth century university graduates had been 1 per 25,000 of the population. By 1855–65 they had fallen to 1 per 77,000 [110: 3]. Roy Lowe calculates that by 1871 there were 3,690 students at Oxford and Cambridge, 300 at London and 1,270 in the provincial civic universities: say, 5,260 students in total [115: 45]. Accordingly the rather subdued role of the English universities in this period at least avoided the over-production of graduates that characterised German and French society. In both Germany and France the relative cheapness of higher education (compared with Oxford and Cambridge), the large number of students, the lure and prestige of civil service employment raising expectations which for many would not be fulfilled, the slow growth of European industry, all helped to create the kind of intellectual disaffection with 'the system' which was an element in the continental revolutions of 1848 and which England was spared [116].

5 Aspirations and Ideologies

The developments we have considered so far were either nationally quite widespread and powerful movements or were concerned with old established institutions. Running through this period, however, were a number of movements or interest groupings whose importance was greater than the actual number of schools and colleges they created. They often pointed the way to future developments or articulated some ideology challenging the prevailing view of education and society. Here we divide them in broad terms into radicals and feminists.

(i) POLITICAL RADICALS

The English radical tradition in the late eighteenth and early nineteenth centuries owed much to the French philosophers who attributed a central importance to education. They in turn saw the English philosopher, John Locke, as a fountainhead of their views. Locke had emphasised that the mind was originally a blank, a *tabula rasa*, and that its ideas were formed by the external impressions presented to it through the senses. These sensations created intellect and character and men were largely what education and environment, as the chief providers of these sensations, made them. These views were taken up and carried to more extreme lengths by French admirers of Locke in the eighteenth century. Helvétius, who had a strong influence in England best expressed this in his famous phrase, 'l'education peut tout'. There was a belief that, as individuals could have their characters formed for them by education, so society itself could be improved and even perfected by a well-designed education system shaping its citizens. The idea of progress turned, with some thinkers like Condorcet, into the idea of perfectibility. Education was thus seen as the key to social engineering and the philosophical ideas of Locke, received and heightened by the French, were re-transmitted back into England. They influenced Tom Paine (*Rights of Man*, 1791) who injected a commitment to education into popular politics, and William Godwin (*Political Justice*, 1793). But most of all they influenced Jeremy Bentham and his followers and Robert Owen.

For Bentham the purpose of social organisation was happiness, 'the greatest happiness of the greatest number', an idea also found in Helvétius [117]. Happiness was best achieved by individuals following their own best interest guided by a seeking of what gave pleasure and an avoidance of pain – his 'felicific calculus'. By and large this rational choice was best exercised by individuals untrammelled by state interference. Yet in certain areas, notably public health, poor law reform and education, Benthamites advocated the necessity of strong state intervention to shape public attitudes and policy. These were all areas where an individual's perception of what may be pleasurable – not taking pains to dispose of refuse, seek work or become literate – did not lead to the correct result of happiness for all. They all required state intervention to provide facilities and penalties which could alter this false perception. This was not an unusual exception. Contemporary classical economists while in most matters espousing *laissez-faire* were also forceful advocates of state intervention in education [118][119]; it was so with Adam Smith, James Mill and Malthus among others [120: *Ch. 8*]. The saving of expense on the social effects of crime or over-population was regarded as an offset against any additional expenditure on the education of the poor. For Bentham the criminal connection was clear, for 'education is only government acting by means of the domestic magistrate'. Accordingly Bentham is seen as a root of both Victorian individualism and liberalism on the one hand and on the other of a coercive welfare state with its paraphernalia of commissions, reports, inspectors and penalties. The other contribution of Bentham himself was the assertion that education should be useful, work-orientated and indeed utilitarian. His only written work on education, *Chrestomathia* (1816), embodied this view.

Bentham was not only important for the ideas associated with his name but also for the inspiration he gave to a group of followers who were to carry these ideas into a whole range of practical educational endeavours. Such men were James Mill, Joseph Hume, Arthur Roebuck and Henry Brougham. There were five main areas in which Benthamites took a leading part. Firstly, they were very active in the infant school movement in London, Brougham setting up the Westminster Infants School in 1818. Secondly, there was a strong Benthamite wing in the Lancasterian movement; James Mill was on the main committee and helped to run the West London Lancasterian Association. Thirdly, it was the Benthamites, notably Brougham and Hume and Jeremy himself, who were behind the formation of University College London in 1826. Fourthly, the concern for practical vocational education was seen in Brougham's support of the mechanics' institute movement in London and the provinces and in the creation of the Society for the Diffusion of Useful Knowledge to provide literature for use in such institutes. Finally, it was the Benthamite group in Parliament – Brougham, Hume, Roebuck, Grote – who over a generation pressed the cause of state intervention in the education of the lower orders. Their pressures ultimately secured the review of charities in the 1820s, surveys of the state of education in 1816, 1818 and 1833, the state grant of 1833 and Committee of Council of 1839.

Robert Owen, like Bentham, attributed the greatest importance to education [121]. For him, men were what they were made in infancy and infants had their characters formed by the sense impressions over which they had no control. The correct education by so forming individuals could create the ideal societies in which they could live happily, for 'it is only by education, rightly understood, that communities of men can ever be well governed, and by means of education every object of human society will be attained'. There were many points of similarity between Owen and Bentham. Both were atheist materialists and influenced by French thinkers, notably Helvétius and Condorcet, and in Owen's case by Rousseau [122]. They both had first-hand experience of Continental developments from journeys there, Bentham to Russia in 1786, Owen to Switzerland in 1818. They both favoured the Lancasterian movement, while Bentham's supporters of the infant school movement were influenced by the Owenite example. Both wanted the state to take some responsibility for the education of the people and both regarded happiness as the ultimate goal of man's endeavours. Bentham even had a financial interest in Owen's factory at New Lanark.

Yet whatever similarities of outlook they shared, they differed sharply over the issue of self-interest. For Bentham, as for the classical economists, self-interest was the legitimate driving force of human society. For Owen it was an evil to be eradicated, the cause of 'all the divisions of mankind, the endless errors and mischiefs of class, sect . . . and all the crimes and misery with which the human race have been hitherto afflicted' [123: *173*]. Education had to counteract this and replace it with the desire for mutual co-operation. This difference over individual interest also reflects the different views of society held by both thinkers. Bentham's preoccupation was with the self-motivated individual: Owen's with men living in communities.

Owen's influence on the education system was threefold, through infant, factory and adult education. Owen opened his infant school at his factory at New Lanark in 1809. Infants began as soon as they could walk and stayed until the age of seven to save them from the influence of their parents. There was a great emphasis on the playground and spontaneous play, on pictures, stories and outings as 'reading readiness'. The ideas gained currency as James Buchanan, Owen's infant master, left New Lanark for London in 1819. There he met Brougham and Samuel Wilderspin who managed an infant school in Spitalfields established by Benthamites already influenced by New Lanark. In 1824 the London Infant School Society was established and Wilderspin toured the country urging the foundation of such schools [124]. He was successful especially in the north where they were valuable in providing some education for children most of whose childhood was to be spent in factory work. Secondly, Owen was a pioneer of the factory schools. These date from 1816 at New Lanark with pupils attending five and a half hours a day as well as performing their factory work [125: *84*]. Many other industrialists, especially in Lancashire where Owen was well known and respected, imitated his experiment. These activities of Owen and his followers made possible the 1833 Factory Act which made the education of factory children obligatory. Thirdly, Owen influenced adult education. His New Institute for the Formation of Character provided not only for children but also for adults and adult education became an important element in the Owenite co-operative communities of the 1820s and 1830s.

There were close interconnections between Benthamites and Owenites in ideology, personal relationships and some practical activities (notably infant schools). Furthermore both benefited from the support and collaboration of Evangelicals in the 1810s and 1820s. In these early decades Anglican Evangelicals were willing to work with a gamut of atheist Philosophical Radicals and Owenites, and Dissenters on schemes of education and social improvement. From the mid-1830s such collaboration tended to break down. As legal disabilities against Catholics and Dissenters were removed, 1828–35, so Anglicans regarded non-Anglicans with increasing suspicion and swung politically to the Right. It undermined radical initiatives like the infant schools and the mechanics institutes and heightened hostility to the University of London [124].

In the 1830s the Chartists joined the Owenite co-operators as a major expression of working-class radicalism and they too had a strong commitment to education [126]. Indeed, one of the aims of the London Workingmen's Association in 1836 had been the fight for a cheap press. Chartists believed in education as a social right just as much as in manhood suffrage. In fact they were linked aims for some Chartists, since working men could not be regarded as fit to exercise political power without a greater degree of education than they already received. William Lovett elaborated Chartist views of education during his imprisonment in 1839–40. He wanted state provision of schools but with teachers appointed by locally elected committees. In addition he envisaged Chartist Halls for lectures, reading rooms and museums. As well as the normal academic subjects, with a strong element of science, there was to be special attention to moral training and the development of social and political awareness in children. This strong emphasis on education by Lovett and the 'moral force' Chartists was mistrusted by the 'physical force' men as diverting attention from their political aims and posing an education hurdle before suffrage could be claimed as a right. What the Chartists actually contributed to the education system in practice is more problematic and is rather a feature of the 1840s than the 1830s. A National Hall was opened in Holborn which became a Chartist Sunday School and then a day school from 1848 until its financial demise in 1857. There also seem to have been schools associated with Chartist Halls in Nottingham, Birmingham, Manchester, Elland, Leicester and Oldham. Silver considers that they 'opened in many places . . . though the extent of the provision of schools by Chartists is far from clear' [127: 83].

The failure of Chartism after its mass demonstration in 1848 gave rise to the Christian Socialist movement. They were Churchmen and others who had been dismayed at the alienation of the radical working classes from Christianity that had been evident during the

Chartist period. The new group wished to demonstrate to working men and ex-Chartists that the religion and Church they had rejected really did care about their aspirations and social reform. Charles Kingsley, Thomas Hughes and F. D. Maurice were among those effecting this fusion of Christianity and radicalism which they termed Christian Socialism. Education inevitably became one of their preoccupations. In 1854 they established their Working Men's College in London with Maurice as principal [128]. Several similar colleges were established by sympathetic clergymen in Sheffield and Nottingham (which slightly preceded the London one), Ancoats, Salford, Wolverhampton, Cambridge, Oxford, Halifax and Leicester. They variously ran libraries and reading rooms, elementary classes and cultural lectures and in the 1870s merged into the wider university extension movement.

Richard Johnson discerns a turning point around 1850. The radicals valued education and knowledge 'often with a quite abstract passion'. Before 1850 they were concerned to try to create their own forms of alternative education outside that provided by the state, and embodying and transmitting their own ideas. From about 1850 with the decline of Chartism this, admittedly expensive and not very successful, 'strategy of substitution' gave way to radical demands for improved facilities for the working classes within the state system [129].

(ii) FEMINISM AND THE EDUCATION OF WOMEN

The education of women and girls had been an issue in England at least from the 1790s and the writing of Mary Wollstonecraft. She claimed equality of education with boys as a means of securing independence for women and capacity to work. Certain social pressures gave these theoretical claims an extra urgency by the mid nineteenth century. Women were still less well educated than men. Although the disparity in their literacy rates had been narrowing since the later eighteenth century, female literacy rates in 1851 were still only 54.8 per cent compared with 69.3 per cent for men. The proportion of women in the population was steadily rising from 1,036 females per 1,000 males in 1821 to 1,054 per 1,000 in 1871. There were 202,400 more women than men of the most marriageable ages of 20–35 in 1841 and by 1871 the surplus had risen to

262,300. Accordingly, over a quarter of a million women had little expectation of marriage and the lifetime protection of husband and home. The situation was exacerbated by the tendency for young men to postpone marriage in order to accumulate capital and establish themselves in their careers. The age of marriage was rising, which also left more single women waiting for, and often never achieving, marriage [130]. Since such women would also have no children they could not look to offspring to support them in old age. Daughters raised in comfortable circumstances also faced other demographic pressures. The increasing size of families with more children surviving diminished the likelihood of a substantial inheritance, while the advancing age of their parents at death deferred that inheritance until later in the daughter's own life. With more women detached in their expectations from reliance on parents or putative husbands and children, they were forced to think in terms of earning their own living in a career. This brought the education issue to the forefront of feminist thinking [131].

Both the education and the opportunities were limited in the first half of the century. Well-to-do girls would be educated at home or at small academies such as 'Miss Pinkerton's' in *Vanity Fair*. The academic content was low and, with the transformation of the grammar school, girls found themselves excluded from such establishments which they had attended in the eighteenth century. Lower-class girls attended the National or British schools along with boys and were destined, if not for the drudgery of a working-class marriage, then for factory work or the vast army of domestic service. The education received by working-class girls in such schools before 1870 was unremarkable and followed the same curriculum as that of the boys, with the probable addition of some sewing and knitting. The concern to develop a more distinctive curriculum for working-class girls with an emphasis on domestic science, cooking, laundry and needlework came after 1870 and especially in the 1880s and 1890s. The problem in the 1840–70 period was largely a middle-class one of finding careers for unmarried middle-class ladies and of fashioning an education which would fit them for them. Around 1850 existing careers were limited and becoming a governess was the only means of earning her livelihood open to the woman of gentle birth. Indeed by 1851 there were some 25,000 governesses in England. Yet they had no proper training and often an education barely above the accomplishments.

Moreover there were uneasy status incongruities. Hired to impart ladylike qualities to her charges, the governess by taking paid employment forfeited her own status as a lady [132].

To meet this situation the Governesses' Benevolent Institution was formed in 1843 to help active governesses to seek posts and aged ones to live in retirement. They tackled the central problem of education by founding Queen's College, Harley Street, in 1848, the prime mover being the Christian Socialist, F. D. Maurice [133]. A highly academic curriculum was developed including the sciences and languages as well as the basic subjects and accomplishments (drawing, music, dancing, needlework). There were also evening lectures for practising governesses as well as the full-time day school work. It was a conscious reaction against the 'Miss Pinkertons' who had left generations of middle-class girls vulnerable with an educa-tion designed to charm a potential husband but ill-suited to running a household or a career. A similar institution, Bedford College, opened in 1849.

Queen's College, Harley Street, was not only important in its own right but also its pupils influenced many areas of feminist life in the 1860s and 1870s. The *English Woman's Journal*, the Social Science Association, the early suffrage and married women's prop-erty movements all owed much to women connected with Queen's. Matilda Bishop (the first Principal of the Royal Holloway College), Frances Dove (the first headmistress of St Leonards), Sophia Jex Blake (the first English doctor) and Octavia Hill (the social work pioneer), were all ex-Queen's students. But most important were Miss Beale and Miss Buss.

In 1858 Dorothea Beale took over the recently founded Chelten-ham Ladies College which was then in a feeble state [134]. She turned it into the model of the high-quality girls' boarding school. Herself a mathematician and logician, she insisted upon a rigorous academic curriculum with an emphasis on mathematics, history and Latin. External examiners were brought in from the universities including Lewis Carroll from Oxford. It became a boarding school in 1864 and an exemplar for its followers, St Leonards and Roedean which were founded after 1870. If Dorothea Beale created the girls' public boarding school, her friend, Frances Mary Buss, created the girls' grammar school. Miss Buss's North London Collegiate School began in 1850 in Camden Town to meet the problem of the lack of education for middle-class girls. Since Miss Buss valued home life in the upbringing of girls it deliberately remained a day school. As at Cheltenham a curriculum including the masculine subjects of science and Latin was followed to emphasise the break with accomplishments.

The North London Collegiate might have remained merely a unique institution associated with its founder had not the feminist educators brought two powerful factors into play. The first of these was the opening of public examinations to girls. Oxford and Cambridge had started Local Examinations for boys' schools in 1858, providing an external common standard. The Victorians laid great stress upon examinations as a means of raising academic performance, deciding the fitness of candidates for public office and as vehicles of social mobility. The feminists saw clearly that external examinations were vital to their cause. Only by publicly matching the standard demanded of boys could the new academic girls' education be taken seriously and throw off the associations of 'soft option' accomplishments that clung to the education of middle-class girls before the 1850s. Accordingly Emily Davies, the future founder of Girton College and sister of a Principal of Queen's College, urged Cambridge to admit girls to its Locals, which it did experimentally from 1863. Miss Buss sent 25 candidates from the North London Collegiate in that year. Following the success of this, Local school examinations were formally opened to girls by Cambridge, Edinburgh and Durham universities in 1865 and 1866. Oxford followed in 1870.

The second factor in the strengthening and spread of girls' education was the securing of financial aid through endowments [135]. In the 1860s the Taunton Commission was examining the endowments for grammar schools. The feminists saw this as another crucial opportunity. Emily Davies insisted that the Commission should examine girls' education, contrary to their original intention. She, Dorothea Beale and Mary Buss gave evidence before it and Miss Beale edited the volume of the report devoted to girls. The Commission resulted in the Endowed Schools Act of 1869 and the creation of the Endowed Schools Commissioners to reform the grammar school endowments. The effect of their work was to reallocate funds from boys' schools or non-educational charities for the benefit of girls. They created 47 new grammar schools between 1869 and 1875 and their successors, the Charity Commission, created another 47 after 1875. Fittingly the North London Collegiate gained an endowment from the reorganisation.

It was inevitable that some of the girls moving through the new academic secondary education would want to pass on to higher education. The early movement for this and its outcome occupied the 1860s. The prime mover was Emily Davies. She wanted higher education for women to widen the range of occupations open to them, fit them for public life, raise the standard of teaching in girls' schools, advance the cause of women's suffrage and match the experience of France, Germany, and Italy where women were accepted into universities. To this end she took a house in Hitchin in 1869 to prepare girls for Cambridge examinations. In 1873 they moved to Cambridge itself as Girton College. At the same time Anne Clough, a governess who had created the North of England Council for the Promotion of the Higher Education of Women in 1867, moved to Cambridge in 1871 to set up what was to become Newnham College. The young women of Girton, at Miss Davies's insistence, were to take only the same examinations as the male undergraduates, whereas at Newnham girls were accepted to take school examinations like the Locals. Girton had the reputation of being a rather uncompromising militant women's rights college, a spearhead in 'the cause'. Emily Davies's problem was that she initially received support from a number of male dons who were rather more interested in curricular reform than women's rights and wished to see Girton as an experiment in this former direction. Davies had to make clear that she was interested in nothing less than that the full curriculum available to men should be made equally available to her girls [136]. Outside Cambridge, Owens College in Manchester admitted women for the first time in 1869. These events closely clustered around 1869–73 were of great importance in their timing since when the civic universities began in the 1870s they accepted the admission of women as a normal policy, while London followed suit in 1878 and Oxford began its belated formation of women's colleges from 1879.

Gillian Sutherland has analysed the social origins and occupations of those first women who attended Girton and Newnham at Cambridge and Somerville and Lady Margaret Hall at Oxford 1869–80. Nearly three-quarters are unknown. Of the rest, 28.6 per cent were daughters of Anglican clergymen, 19.6 per cent had fathers in commerce, 14.3 per cent were daughters of academics and schoolmasters, 9.8 per cent had fathers in industry, 7.1 per cent were daughters of lawyers and the same percentage daughters of doctors, and 6.2 per cent had landed fathers. The strong element of fathers in commerce and industry is the more remarkable in that the colleges did not attract benefactions from the wealthiest sectors of such classes. More predictably 93 per cent of those known to have gained employment became teachers [137].

The impetus behind the higher education of women was confused by its dual market. On the one hand there were ladies seeking culture but not careers. On the other were women of more modest origins and expectations who needed jobs to sustain a livelihood, usually as schoolteachers. The state saw no need to subsidise the former and private benefactors had little enthusiasm for the latter. Such negative attitudes counteracted the otherwise strong motives for women's education and kept women's colleges underfunded [138].

These strivings of women to gain acceptance for their claims for education had to face considerable opposition [139]. A whole gamut of arguments was arrayed against them. It was held that women were of inferior intellect to men – craniometry studies in the 1860s suggested that their brains were smaller – and so incapable of the same education. Even worse, it was believed that the strain imposed by mental activity would stunt their sexual development leading to sterility and a decline of the birth rate. The same outcome would be the result of newly educated women following careers, gaining financial independence and spurning marriage. Moreover, highly educated women would increase the applicants for high status occupations and depress the middle-class job market which would further diminish the ability of middle-class men to earn salaries sufficient to support families. At the end of many of these chains of arguments advanced by male social critics was the spectre of the 'mannish' woman and the collapsing middle-class birth rate. The fact that only about a quarter of the early Girton and Lady Margaret Hall graduates actually did marry would have been seen by them as confirming their worst fears. However, the beneficial effects of women's education are inestimable. All the expectations voiced by Emily Davies came to fruition. British society was enriched by able and intelligent women in the professions (notably in grammar school teaching), in public life and in service on committees in a range of activities from School Boards to the plethora of charitable organisations that marked late Victorian England. Above all, self-confident and self-respecting, they looked forward eagerly for the vote.

Conclusion

Historians of education tend to stress the achievements and development of education in this period, yet economic historians, especially those with a bias towards formal economics and an interest in growth, take a cooler view. They point out that Britain's rapid economic growth in this classic period of the industrial revolution was achieved with very modest levels of human capital. We have noted a substantial body of original research (Schofield, Sanderson, Laqueur, Nicholas, etc.) which found that stagnant or declining literacy underlay the 'revolution' of the late eighteenth and early nineteenth century. A little later Sandberg has noted that Britain in 1850 was the wealthiest country in the world but only in the second rank as regards literacy levels. N. F. R. Crafts has shown that in 1870 when again Britain was the world economic leader, its school enrolment ratio was only 0.168 compared with the European norm of 0.514 and 'Britain persistently had a relatively low rate of accumulation of human capital'. [140]. Not that this seemed to matter. The fullest study of long-term economic growth in this period came to the conclusion that between 1856 and 1873 improvements in education contributed only 0.3 per cent per year to the growth in labour quality (0.2 per cent for formal school education, 0.1 per cent for technical education, nil for university education) [23].

The conjunction of economic success with modest levels of educational achievement and human capital cast dangerous shadows forward into the future. Stephen Nicholas after his study of declining literacy considered that 'Britain may have had adequate human capital inputs in the pre-1850 period, but the habit of under-investing in human capital was one of the most pervasive industrial revolution legacies.' Margaret Gowing was similarly critical: 'Britain had achieved so much in the early nineteenth century with so little education that she felt no need to create the educational infrastructure which her potential competitors were building'. [141].

How far was 1870 a turning point? The date is associated with the Forster Education Act of that year and accordingly has acquired a rather exaggerated status. The 1870 Act introduced secular, rate-supported elementary schools administered by about 2,000 School Boards and occasioned a renewed impetus in school building, yet it hardly created the elementary school system in England. The bulk of the work had already been accomplished by the Church schools from the 1830s. The literacy rate was already high and required only a further topping-up to raise it from the 80s to the 90s in percentage terms.

Yet 1870 was a turning point not so much in elementary education as in other spheres. In the 1870s the post-Taunton Commissioners were creating the new generation of grammar schools, including those for girls, which were to have a profound effect in creating the late-Victorian middle classes. The 1870s were also decisive for the universities. The Cleveland Commission (1875) began much of the essential modernisation of Oxford and Cambridge. The 1870s also saw the reception of women into the ancient universities while reciprocally a new outgoing spirit was manifest at Cambridge in the university extension movement, providing lectures in the provinces. Even more important the 1870s saw the formation of many of the civic universities in the North and the Midlands, no longer in thrall to 'liberal education' but in tune with the industrial and professional needs of their areas [142]. Also in the 1870s, following the Paris Exhibition, came a new need to take technical education seriously. In 1870 these matters lay in the near future and beyond the scope of this study. Yet the years following 1870 were to be even more fruitful for these more advanced forms of education than for the elementary schooling for which 1870 is regarded as a significant point of departure.

Overall, 1870 marked a watershed in two main shifts of emphasis. From the 1830s to 1870 the main thrust of public policy had been the response to a social problem created by successful industrialisation, namely the mass education of the working classes. After 1870 the aspirations of the working classes themselves rose from the securing of a basic literacy education to the desire for some form of secondary instruction. Secondly, and most importantly, the main effort of educational development shifted towards trying to create an education system which would not only deal with a social problem at home but which would sustain the economy in the face of competition abroad from the industries of Germany and the United States of America.

Select Bibliography

The literature is vast but the bibliography must be as severely selective as the text. The best textbooks which start their coverage in the eighteenth century are:

J. W. Adamson, *English Education 1789–1902* (Cambridge, 1930).

H. C. Barnard, *A Short History of English Education from 1760* (London, 1947).

The two leading monographs covering the period are:

Brian Simon, *Studies in the History of Education 1780–1870* (London, 1960).

J. S. Hurt, *Education in Evolution 1800–1870* (London, 1971).

Useful collections of documents with commentary and bibliographies are:

Ann Digby and Peter Searby, *Children, School and Society in Nineteenth Century England* (London, 1981) on schooling.

Michael Sanderson, *The Universities in the Nineteenth Century* (London, 1975) on higher education.

The chief English research journals are *History of Education, British Journal of Educational Studies, Journal of Educational Administration and History*, only a few of whose valuable articles can be referred to below.

The *Economic History Review* makes an annual review of periodical literature including a section on education. *EcHR* in the References refers to the second series of the *Review*.

LITERACY AND ELEMENTARY EDUCATION BEFORE 1830

[1]   Roger Schofield, 'The Measurement of Literacy in Pre-Industrial England', in Jack Goody (ed.), *Literacy in Traditional Societies* (Cambridge, 1968).

[2] M. G. Jones, *The Charity School Movement in the Eighteenth Century* (Cambridge, 1938). Major classic but dating in some respects, see [3].

[3] Joan Simon, 'Was there a Charity School Movement? The Leicestershire Evidence', in Brian Simon (ed.) *Education in Leicestershire 1640–1940* (Leicester, 1968). Discounts SPCK involvement in the county.

[4] Derek Robson, *Some Aspects of Education in Cheshire in the Eighteenth Century* (Chetham Soc. 3rd ser., XIII, 1966) App. I. Good regional study.

[5] Marion Johnson, *Derbyshire Village Schools in the Nineteenth Century* (Newton Abbot, 1970).

[6] Michael Sanderson, 'Literacy and Social Mobility in the Industrial Revolution in England', *Past and Present*, 56 (August 1972). A regional modifcation of [8]. It suggests a decline in literacy and agrees with [9].

[7] V. E. Neuburg, *Popular Education in the Eighteenth Century* (London, 1971). Interesting on the literature available for education and self-education in the eighteenth century.

[8] Lawrence Stone, 'Literacy and Education in England 1640–1900', *Past and Present*, 42 (February 1969) pp. 120–1. A major article presenting the view of rising literacy. Equally influential on those who agree [12] and disagree [6] [19].

[9] R. A. Houston, *Scottish Literacy and the Scottish Identity, Illiteracy and Society in Scotland and Northern England 1600–1800* (Cambridge, 1985). Major study and important for England showing rising literacy to 1770s.

[10] W. L. Sargent, 'On the Progress of Elementary Education', *Journal of the Royal Statistical Society* (1867).

[11] W. P. Baker, *Parish Registers and Illiteracy in East Yorkshire* (East Yorkshire Local History Soc. 13, 1961). Important pioneer study.

[12] R. M. Hartwell, 'Education and Economic Growth in England During the Industrial Revolution', *Annales Cisalpines d'Histoire Sociale*, Serie I, N. 2 (Pavia, 1971). Optimist view of rising literacy and education and their relevance for industrialisation.

[13] Thomas W. Laqueur, *Religion and Respectability, Sunday Schools and Working Class Culture 1780–1850* (Yale, 1976).

A work of first-rate importance on a major movement. But see [15].

[14]   A. P. Wadsworth, 'The First Manchester Sunday Schools'. *Bulletin of the John Rylands Library,* xxx (1951). A pioneer essay.

[15]   Malcolm Dick, 'The Myth of the Working Class Sunday School', *History of Education,* vol. 9, 1 (1980). Convincingly sceptical of [13] over its 'working class' claims.

[16]   Thomas W. Laqueur, 'Literacy and Social Mobility in the Industrial Revolution in England', *Past and Present,* 64 (August 1974). Confirms Sanderson's literacy findings in [6] while criticising his arguments about social mobility.

[17]   Frances O'Shaughnessy, *A Spa and its Children* (Warwick, 1979). Local study with some detailed literacy evidence.

[18]   W. B. Stephens, 'Illiteracy in Devon during the Industrial Revolution 1754–1844', *Journal of Educational Administration and History* (January 1976).

[19]   R. S. Schofield, 'Dimensions of Illiteracy 1750–1850', *Explorations in Economic History,* vol. 10, 4 (Summer 1973). Leading statement of the view of literacy stagnation, and sceptical over relevance of literacy. Compare [6] which is in accord.

[20]   Stephen Nicholas, 'Literacy and the Industrial Revolution', in Gabriel Tortella (ed.), *Education and Economic Development since the Industrial Revolution* (Valencia, 1990). Brilliant analysis of fascinating new convict data. 'Pessimistic' conclusion.

[21]   W. B. Stephens, *Education, Literacy and Society 1830–70* (Manchester, 1987). Very good on regional variations.

[22]   David Vincent, *Literacy and Popular Culture in England 1750–1914* (Cambridge, 1989). Some new data and good on how and why literacy was attained.

[23]   R. C. O. Matthews, C. H. Feinstein and J. C. Odling-Smee, *British Economic Growth 1856–1973* (Oxford, 1982).

[24]   Richard Johnson, 'Educational Policy and Social Control in Early Victorian England', *Past and Present,* 49 (November 1970). Influential in helping to create a fashion for the 'social control' concept.

[25]   Philip McCann, 'Popular Education, Socialization and Social Control: Spitalfields 1812–1824', in P. McCann,

Popular Education and Socialization in the Nineteenth Century (London, 1977).

[26] Robert Colls, ' "Oh Happy English Children", Coal, Class and Education in the North East', *Past and Present*, no. 73 (November 1976). Regional example of education as 'social control'.

[27] T. W. Laqueur, 'The Cultural Origins of Popular Literacy in England', *Oxford Review of Education*, vol. 2, 3 (1976). Perceptive on wider uses of literacy in industrial and pre-industrial society.

THE ADVANCE OF SCHOOLING 1830–1870

[28] J. M. Goldstrom, *The Social Content of Education 1808–1870* (Irish Universities Press, 1972). Very good on school literature. Also on finance.

[29] E. G. West 'Resource Allocation and Growth in Early Nineteenth-Century British Education', *Economic History Review*, xxiii, 1 (April 1970). An interesting calculation for the 1830s, though criticised by J. S. Hurt, *EcHR*, xxiv, 4 (November 1971).

[30] D. G. Paz, *The Politics of Working Class Education 1830–50* (Manchester, 1980). Best new analysis of politics of state intervention.

[31] Richard Johnson, 'Administrators in Education before 1870: Patronage, Social Position and Role', in Gillian Sutherland, *Studies in the Growth of Nineteenth Century Government* (London, 1972). Influential on the 'administrator as statesman' idea.

[32] D. W. Sylvester, *Robert Lowe and Education* (Cambridge, 1974). Reassessment of Lowe as caring Benthamite rather than reactionary retrencher.

[33] Mary Sturt, *The Education of the People* (London, 1967). Dating, but still best treatment covering the whole of the nineteenth century.

[34] E. G. West, 'Literacy and the Industrial Revolution', *Economic History Review*, xxxi, 3 (August 1978).

[35] T. W. Laqueur, 'Working Class Demand and the Growth of English Elementary Education 1750–1850', in L. Stone (ed.),

Schooling and Society (Johns Hopkins, Baltimore, 1976). Interesting on private schools for working class.

[36] Philip W. Gardner, *The Lost Elementary Schools of Victorian England* (London, 1984). Convincing argument for importance of private working-class schooling. See [35].

[37] Asher Tropp, *The Schoolteachers* (London, 1957).

[38] Nancy Ball, *Her Majesty's Inspectorate 1839–1849* (University of Birmingham Institute of Education, 1963).

[39] H. W. Schupf, 'Education for the Neglected: Ragged Schools in Nineteenth Century England', *History of Education Quarterly* (Summer 1972).

[40] Michael Sanderson, 'Education and the Factory in Industrial Lancashire 1780–1840', *Economic History Review*, xx (1967).

[41] R. K. Webb, *The British Working Class Reader 1790–1848: Literacy and Social Tension* (London, 1955).

[42] Patricia Hollis, *The Pauper Press* (Oxford, 1970).

[43] R. D. Altick, *The English Common Reader, a Social History of the Mass Reading Public 1800–1900* (Chicago, 1957).

[44] H. J. Burgess, *Enterprise in Education* (London, 1958). Useful history of the National Society up to 1870.

[45] W. P. McCann, 'Elementary Education in England and Wales on the Eve of the 1870 Education Act', *Journal of Educational Administration and History* (December 1969).

[46] Lars G. Sandberg, 'Ignorance, Poverty and Economic Backwardness', *The Journal of European Economic History*, vol. II, no. 3 (Winter 1982). Interesting international comparison of literacy and GNP ratings.

SCIENTIFIC CULTURE IN THE EIGHTEENTH CENTURY

[47] Irene Parker, *Dissenting Academies in England* (Cambridge, 1914). Still valuable, the best short treatment. [48] and [50] extend the data.

[48] H. McLachlan, *English Education under the Test Acts* (Manchester, 1931).

[49] Nicholas Hans, *New Trends in Education in the Eighteenth Century* (London, 1951). Good on science teachers in the eighteenth century.

[50] J. W. Ashley Smith, *The Birth of Modern Education, the Contribution of the Dissenting Academies 1660–1800* (London, 1954). Useful on theological background to scientific thought.

[51] H. McLachlan, *Warrington Academy, its History and Influence* (Chetham Soc. New Ser., vol. 107, 1943).

[52] A. E. Musson and E. Robinson, 'Science and Industry in the Late Eighteenth Century', in *Science and Technology in the Industrial Revolution* (Manchester, 1969). Influential statement of importance of scientific subculture.

[53] Diana Harding, 'Mathematics and Science Education in Eighteenth Century Northamptonshire', *History of Education* (June 1972). Like [54][55], valuable regional extension of [52].

[54] Trevor Fawcett, 'Popular Science in Eighteenth Century Norwich', *History Today*, vol. 22 (1972).

[55] Ian Inkster, 'Culture, Institutions and Urbanity: The Itinerant Science Lecturer in Sheffield 1790–1850', in S. Pollard and C. Holmes (eds), *Essays in the Economic and Social History of South Yorkshire* (Sheffield, 1976).

[56] Robert E. Schofield, *The Lunar Society of Birmingham* (Oxford, 1963).

[57] G. W. Roderick and M. D. Stephens, *Scientific and Technical Education in Nineteenth Century England* (Newton Abbot, 1972). Useful essays on Liverpool and Cornwall.

[58] W. H. G. Armytage, 'Education and Innovative Ferment in England 1588–1805', in C. A. Anderson and M. Bowman (eds), *Education and Economic Development* (Chicago, 1965).

[59] D. G. C. Allan, *William Shipley, Founder of the Royal Society of Arts* (London, 1968).

[60] Morris Berman, *Social Change and Scientific Organisation, the Royal Institution 1799–1844* (Ithaca, N. York, 1978).

[61] R. S. Porter, 'Science, Provincial Culture and Public Opinion in Enlightenment England', *British Journal of Eighteenth Century Studies*, vol. 3, no. 1 (Spring 1980).

[62] David Wykes, 'Sons and Subscribers: Lay Support and the College 1786–1840', in Barbara Smith (ed.), *Truth Liberty Religion, Essays Celebrating Two Hundred Years of Manchester College* (Oxford, 1986).

[63] A. and N. Clow, *The Chemical Revolution* (London, 1952). On Scottish science, industry and culture.

MECHANICS' INSTITUTES AND TECHNICAL EDUCATION

[64] Thomas Kelly, *George Birkbeck, Pioneer of Adult Education* (Liverpool, 1957). Excellent biography.

[65] Thomas Kelly, *A History of Adult Education in Great Britain* (Liverpool, 1962). The best overall study of adult education.

[66] Mabel Tylecote, *The Mechanics' Institutes of Lancashire and Yorkshire Before 1851* (Manchester, 1957).

[67] J. F. C. Harrison, *Learning and Living 1790–1960* (London, 1961). Especially good on Yorkshire before 1914.

[68] Edward Royle, 'Mechanics' Institutes and the Working Classes 1840–60', *Historical Journal*, XIV, 2 (1971). Stresses non-technical value of institutes to working classes. Compare [69].

[69] Ian Inkster, 'The Social Context of an Educational Movement: A Revisionalist Approach to the English Mechanics' Institutes', *Oxford Review of Education*, vol. 2, 3 (1976). Emphasises middle-class element of movement.

[70] D. S. L. Cardwell, *The Organisation of Science in England* (London, 1972). Best overall study of nineteenth-century technical and scientific education.

[71] G. W. Tracey, 'The Origin and Growth of Scientific Instruction in Science Classes under the Science and Art Department 1858–1870', *Durham Research Review*, V, 21 (September 1968).

GRAMMAR AND PRIVATE SCHOOLS

[72] J. H. Plumb, 'The New World of Children in the Eighteenth Century', *Past and Present*, 67 (May 1975).

[73] Zena Cook and Brian Simon, 'Private Schools in Leicester and the County 1780–1840', in Brian Simon (ed.), *Education in Leicestershire 1540–1940* (Leicester, 1968).

[74] Richard S. Tompson, *Classics or Charity? The Dilemma of the Eighteenth Century Grammar School* (Manchester, 1971). Careful statistical analysis of an important social change.

[75] John Roach, *Public Examinations in England 1850–1900* (Cambridge, 1971).

[76] F. E. Balls, 'The Endowed Schools Act 1869 and the Development of the English Grammar School in the Nineteenth Century', *Durham Research Review*, v, 19 (September 1967), 20 (April 1968).

THE PUBLIC SCHOOLS

[77] T. W. Bamford, *The Rise of the Public Schools* (London, 1967). The best overall treatment.

[78] J. R. de S. Honey, *Tom Brown's Universe, the Development of the Victorian Public School* (London, 1977). A wider range of interesting themes than [77], which it complements.

[79] F. Musgrove, 'Middle Class Families and School 1780–1880: Interaction and Exchange of Function between Institutions', *Sociological Review* (December 1959).

[80] John Chandos, *Boys Together, English Public Schools 1800–1864* (Oxford, 1985). Lively account of pre-reform schools.

[81] A. J. Meadows and W. H. Brock, 'Topics Fit for Gentlemen: The Problem of Science in the Public School Curriculum', in Brian Simon and Ian Bradley (eds), *The Victorian Public School* (London, 1975).

[82] David Newsome, *Godliness and Good Learning* (London, 1961). Fascinating on changing public school ethos.

[83] J. A. Mangan, *Athleticism in the Victorian and Edwardian Public School* (Cambridge, 1981).

[84] Geoffrey Best, 'Militarism and the Victorian Public School', in *The Victorian Public School*; see [81].

[85] T. W. Bamford, 'Public Schools and Social Class 1801–1850', *British Journal of Sociology*, xii (1961).

[86] J. H. Bishop and Rupert Wilkinson, *Winchester and the Public School Elite* (London, 1967). Penetrating historical

sociological analysis. Its insights deserve to be better known to non-educational historians.

[87] D. C. Coleman, 'Gentlemen and Players', *Economic History Review*, XXVI, 1 (1973).

[88] Donald Leinster-Mackay, *The Rise of the English Prep School* (London, 1984).

[89] W. J. Reader, *Professional Men* (London, 1966) App. 2: 'Public Schoolboys' Occupations 1807–1911'.

[90] Y. Cassis, 'Bankers in English Society in the late Nineteenth Century', *Economic History Review*, 2nd series, XXVIII, no. 2 (1985).

[91] Martin J. Wiener, *English Culture and the Decline of the Industrial Spirit 1850–1980* (Cambridge, 1981) p. 154. Very influential and highly readable. Attributes industrial decline to psychological-cultural factors in which education bears some culpability.

[92] F. Musgrove, 'Middle Class Education and Employment in the Nineteenth Century', *Economic History Review*, XII, 1 (1959–60). Its figures were rightly criticised by Harold Perkin in *EcHR*, XIV, 1 (1961) but its main social point is still valid.

OXFORD, CAMBRIDGE AND LIBERAL EDUCATION

[93] Lawrence Stone, 'The Size and Composition of the Oxford Student Body 1580–1910', in L. Stone (ed.), *The University in Society*, vol. 1 (Princeton, 1975).

[94] C. A. Anderson and Miriam Schnaper, *School and Society in England, Social Backgrounds of Oxford and Cambridge Students* (Washington, 1952). With [95], indispensable sociological analysis of Georgian–Victorian Oxford and Cambridge.

[95] Hester Jenkins and D. Caradog Jones, 'The Social Class of Cambridge University Alumni of the 18th and 19th Centuries', *British Journal of Sociology*, vol. 1 (1950).

[96] Roy M. Macleod, 'Resources of Science in Victorian England: The Endowment of Science Movement 1868–1900 in Peter Mathias (ed.), *Science and Society 1600–1900*

(Cambridge, 1972). Valuable on the 'research' idea in universities.

[97]   Sheldon Rothblatt, *The Revolution of the Dons, Cambridge and Society in Victorian England* (London, 1968).

[98]   ———————— *Tradition and Change in English Liberal Education* (London, 1976).

[99]   Robert G. McPherson, *Theory of Higher Education in Nineteenth Century England* (University of Georgia, 1959). Best overall exposition of the nineteenth-century debate on the function of universities.

[100]   Martha McMackin Garland, *Cambridge before Darwin, the Ideal of a Liberal Education* (Cambridge, 1980). Very good on William Whewell.

[101]   A. Dwight Culler, *The Imperial Intellect, a Study of Newman's Educational Ideal* (Yale, 1955).

[102]   F. W. Garforth, *Educative Democracy, John Stuart Mill on Education and Society* (Oxford, 1980).

[103]   Peter Slee, 'The Oxford Idea of a Liberal Education 1800–1860', *History of Universities*, vol. VII (1988).

[104]   J. P. C. Roach (ed.), 'The City and University of Cambridge', in *Victoria County History of Cambridgeshire* (Oxford, 1959).

[105]   W. R. Ward, *Victorian Oxford* (London, 1965).

[106]   G. W. Roderick and M. D. Stephens, 'Scientific Studies at Oxford and Cambridge 1850–1914', *British Journal of Educational Studies* (February 1976).

[107]   A. J. Engel, *From Clergyman to Don, the Rise of the Academic Profession in Nineteenth Century Oxford* (Oxford, 1983).

[108]   Janet Howarth, 'Science Education in Late-Victorian Oxford: A Curious Case of Failure?', *English Historical Review*, vol. CII (1987).

[109]   Harvey W. Becher, 'The Social Origins and Post Graduate Careers of a Cambridge Intellectual Elite 1830–1860', *Victorian Studies*, vol. 28, no. 1 (Autumn 1984).

ALTERNATIVE TRADITIONS

[110]   Michael Sanderson, *The Universities and British Industry 1850–1970* (London, 1972).

[111]   Robert H. Kargon, *Science in Victorian Manchester* (Manchester, 1977).

[112]   Charles Newman, *The Evolution of Medical Education in the Nineteenth Century* (Oxford, 1957).

[113]   Negley Harte, *The University of London 1836–1986* (London, 1986).

[114]   J. P. C. Roach, 'Victorian Universities and the National Intelligentsia', *Victorian Studies* (December 1959).

[115]   Roy Lowe, 'The Expansion of Higher Education in England', in Konrad H. Jaraush (ed.), *The Transformation of Higher Learning 1860–1930* (Chicago, 1983). The best and fullest figures on Victorian higher education.

[116]   Lenore O'Boyle, 'The Problem of Educated Men in Western Europe 1800–1850', *Journal of Modern History*, vol. 42, 4 (December 1970).

RADICALS AND EDUCATION

[117]   Nicholas Hans, 'Bentham and the Utilitarians', in A. V. Judges (ed.), *Pioneers of English Education* (London, 1952).

[118]   Mark Blaug, 'The Economics of Education in English Classical Political Economy: A Re-examination', in *Economic History and the History of Economics* (New York, 1986).

[119]   Richard Johnson, 'Educating the Educator. "Experts" and the State 1833–9', in A. P. Donagrodzki (ed.), *Social Control in Nineteenth Century Britain* (London, 1977).

[120]   E. G. West, *Education and the State* (London, 1965). Good on political economists and education.

[121]   Harold Silver, *The Concept of Popular Education* (London, 1965). Chiefly on Robert Owen.

[122]   Margery Browning, 'Owen as an Educator', in John Butt (ed.), *Robert Owen* (Newton Abbot, 1971)

[123]   Harold Silver (ed.), *Robert Owen on Education* (Cambridge, 1967). Useful extracts from Owen's writings.

[124]   Phillip McCann and Francis A. Young, *Samuel Wilderspin and the Infant School Movement* (London, 1982).

[125]   Karen C. Altfest, *Robert Owen as Educator* (Boston, 1977). Good conspectus view of a theme on which there is much disparate literature.

[126]   Michael Cullen, 'The Chartists and Education', *New Zealand Journal of History*, x, 2 (October 1976).

[127]   Harold Silver, *English Education and the Radicals 1780–1850* (London, 1975).

[128]   J. F. C. Harrison, *A History of the Working Men's College 1854–1954* (London, 1954). On Christian Socialist activity.

[129]   Richard Johnson, '"Really Useful Knowledge": Radical Education and Working Class Culture 1790–1848', in John Clarke (ed.), *Working Class Culture, Studies in History and Theory* (London, 1979).

THE EDUCATION OF WOMEN

[130]   Sara Delamont, 'The Contradictions in Ladies' Education', in Sara Delamont and Lorna Duffin (eds), *The Nineteenth Century Woman, Her Cultural and Physical World* (London, 1978).

[131]   Margaret Bryant, *The Unexpected Revolution: A Study in the History of the Education of Women and Girls in the Nineteenth Century* (London, 1979). The best modern survey.

[132]   M. Jeanne Peterson, 'The Victorian Governess, Status Incongruence in Family and Society', in Martha Vicinus, *Suffer and be Still* (Bloomington, 1972).

[133]   Elaine Kaye, *A History of Queen's College, London, 1848–1972* (London, 1972).

[134]   Josephine Kamm, *How Different from Us: a Biography of Miss Buss and Miss Beale* (London, 1958).

[135]   Sheila Fletcher, *Feminists and Bureaucrats* (Cambridge, 1980). Excellent on Taunton, its subsequent Commissioners and girls' grammar schools.

[136]   Rita McWilliams Tullberg, *Women at Cambridge* (London, 1975).

[137]   Gillian Sutherland, 'The Movement for the Higher Education of Women: Its Social and Intellectual Context in England c1840–80', in P. J. Waller (ed.), *Political and Social Change in Modern Britain* (London, 1987). Valuable discussion and important new statistical data on women students [see 138].

[138] Janet Howarth and Mark Curthoys, 'The Political Economy of Women's Higher Education in Late Nineteenth and Early Twentieth Century Britain', *Historical Research*, vol. 60, no. 142 (June 1987).

[139] Joan N. Burstyn, *Victorian Education and the Ideal of Womanhood* (London, 1980). Good on opposition to the education of women.

CONCLUSION

[140] N. F. R. Crafts, *British Economic Growth During the Industrial Revolution* (Oxford, 1985). A major influential work. Valuable here for its data and comments on education and economic growth. See also [23][46].

[141] Margaret Gowing, 'Science, Technology and Education: England in 1870', *Notes and Records of the Royal Society of London*, vol. 32 (1977–8).

[142] David R. Jones, *The Origins of Civic Universities* (London, 1988).

Addendum:
Since this volume was revised the following important item has become available:

Gillian Sutherland, 'Education', in F. M. L. Thompson (ed.), *The Cambridge Social History of Britain, 1750–1950*, vol. 3 (Cambridge, 1990).

Index

Journal of Natural Philosophy 30

Kay Shuttleworth, Sir James 21, 24
Keir, James 30, 32
Kendal Academy 29, 32
King's College, London 54
Kingsley, Charles 43, 61
Kings Lynn 12
Kirkham 15, 16

laboratory building 48
Lady Margaret Hall, Oxford 65
Lancashire 10, 12, 13, 14, 15, 16, 18, 29, 59
Lancaster, Joseph 21
Lancasterian movement 58
Lancing 41
latent heat 32
Laqueur, T. W. 13, 14, 15, 16, 22
law 44, 51, 54
lead chamber process 32
Leamington Spa 15, 16
Leblanc process 32
Leeds Grammar School 39
Leeds Mechanics' Institute 33
Leeds Medical School 53
Leeds Yorkshire College of Science 35
Leicester Chartist Hall 60
Leicester Working Men's (Vaughan) College 61
Leicestershire 38
Leiden 31
letter writing 20, 26
liberal education 31, 49–51
Liebig, J. von 34
literacy 9–27,
    measurement 9–10; early eighteenth century 10–11; late eighteenth and early nineteenth century 10–18; mid-nineteenth century 18–19; late nineteenth century 69; female 11, 14, 16, 61;

relevance for industrial society 17–18, 20–1; GNP and 27
Literae Humaniores 51
Literary and Philosophical Societies 30
Liverpool Mechanics' Institute 33
Liverpool Medical School 53
local examinations 40, 64
Locke, John 28, 56
London 24, 58
London Infant School Society 59
London Mechanics' Institute 33
London University 53, 54, 58, 65
London Working Men's Association 60
Lovett, William 60
Lowe, Robert 22
Lowe, R. 54
Lunar Society 30

Macmillan, Alexander 42
Malthus, Thomas 25, 57
Malvern 41
Manchester 15, 16, 53
Manchester Academy 29
Manchester Chartist Hall 60
Manchester College 31
Manchester Grammar School 40
Manchester Literary and Philosophical Society 30
Manchester Mechanics' Institute 33
Manchester Medical School 53
Marlborough 41, 43
Marshall, John 33, 44
Martineau, Harriet 25
masons 18
Mathematical Tripos, Cambridge 46
mathematics 25, 46, 47, 48, 50, 63
Maurice, F. D. 61, 63
McCann, Philip 19